Endorsements

"Stroke, stroke, breathe…. Stroke, stroke, breathe… This is the mantra that Paul Asmuth repeated over and over again as he swam his way into the history book of open water swimming. *The Sport of the Soul* chronicles the journey of a man known in the world of competitive swimming simply as "the Legend." I think of Paul as a uniquely gifted aquatic mystic. Marathon swimming is not for the faint of heart. It takes so much more than physical strength and stamina. This book takes the reader into the realm of Spirit, transcending the physical senses to the experience of an infinite Resource that lies within every human being. To me, this book is as much about what it means to be a spiritual seeker as it is about what it took to become the most decorated open water swimmer of his day. I encourage anyone to put on the proverbial Speedo, grab a pair of goggles, lather up with lanolin, and jump into the water with Paul. Suffer the incredible hardship, doubt, and uncertainty one has to face in a 20-plus-mile race. Feel the love and support from the guide boat. Learn from the wisdom of the world's finest coaches. At the finish line, experience the pure joy of accomplishment, the adulation of fans, the gratitude for everything that got you there, and the tears that you can't keep back."

—Reverend William "Father Mac" McIlmoyl
Rector, Grace Church, St. Helena, 1993–2016
Pastor and friend of Paul's for twenty-five years

"The *Traversee du Lac St. Jean* and du Lac Memphremagog are proud to have witnessed one of the greatest marathon swimmers of all time. This book tells the stories behind some of Paul Asmuth's most memorable races, and a story of a man who found a meaning to his life racing in the world's toughest waters. This book gives us an unprecedented look not only at the motivations and challenges that made him such a dominant athlete but also how friendships, faith, and trust have helped him through his amazing journey."

—Jean Arel
Radio-Canada,
Sherbrooke, Quebec, Canada

"Paul Asmuth's legendary marathon swimming career reveals a man grounded in faith, positive energy, and incredible personal strength. Those searching for inspiration and motivation would do well to read this story of a life well lived."

—Bob Bowman
USA Olympic Swimming Coach 2004, 2008, 2012, 2016;
Arizona State University Head Swimming Coach

"In those times when glory seems to exist through the eyes of others, *Marathon Swimming: The Sport of the Soul* brings you back to the only form of glory that really matters. The one that comes from overcoming your own fears and limits. The one that arises within you, from the struggle you've put in."

—Lynn Blouin
Former Race Organizer,
International Marathon Swimming Association
General Secretary
Magog, Quebec, Canada

"Having known Paul as a coach for years, I thoroughly enjoyed learning more about his life journey and athletic background. I've been a lifelong swimmer and have to admit that I know little about the struggles, both mentally and physically, that marathon swimmers endure. Whether you are an athlete or not, you can gain valuable insight from Paul and the mental strategies that he employed to become one of the most accomplished marathon swimmers in history."

—Natalie Coughlin Hall
Twelve-time Olympic swimming medalist;
author, vintner, gardener, and culinary artist

"An amazing story of athletic performance and dedication. Paul Asmuth, arguably one of the best marathon swimmers of all time, takes the reader through the perils and joys of competitive open water swimming. Supported by friends, family, and faith, Paul dominates this brutal sport for close to twenty years. An inspiration for all, this remarkable narrative reveals an unusual degree of determination and pursuit of excellence."

—Donald P. Hill
University of Michigan,
NCAA Swimming Champion,
World and American Record Holder

"Paul's story is honest, fascinating, and, perhaps most important, inspirational. The world of marathon swimming is as strange as it is oddly beautiful. And while it may seem as foreign as the moon to most of us, how Paul deals with triumph and tragedy brings the story right into our hearts and homes."

—KEN MCALPINE
AUTHOR OF *ISLANDS APART:*
A YEAR ON THE EDGE OF CIVILIZATION

"Paul Asmuth honestly interweaves his faith in God with the numerous trials, obstacles, and victories of his Hall of Fame career. He presents an insider's view of the relentlessly challenging world of professional marathon swimming. His detailed recollections of his races and solo swims around the world make readers feel a part of his escort crew. He describes his painful bouts of hypothermia, swims against oncoming currents, and struggles against ocean waves—and how he dug deep while praying to reach the finish. Paul explains key periods of his life where he balances the demands of an extreme athlete at the highest echelon of his sport while working full time as an accountant. It was thoroughly enjoyable to learn about the lifestyle and mind-set of a seven-time world champion."

—STEVEN MUNATONES
FOUNDER OF WORLD OPEN WATER SWIMMING
ASSOCIATION AND KAATSU GLOBAL,
INTERNATIONAL MARATHON SWIMMING HALL OF FAME INDUCTEE

MARATHON SWIMMING
THE SPORT OF THE SOUL

Inspiring Stories of Passion, Faith, and Grit

Paul Andrew Asmuth

ELM HILL

A Division of
HarperCollins Christian Publishing

www.elmhillbooks.com

Marathon Swimming
The Sport Of The Soul
Inspiring Stories of Passion, Faith, and Grit

Published in Nashville, Tennessee, by Elm Hill, an imprint of Thomas Nelson. Elm Hill and Thomas Nelson are registered trademarks of HarperCollins Christian Publishing, Inc.

Cover photo by Marilyn Moe Asmuth, Lac Memphremagog, Saint-Benoit-du-Lac in background

Elm Hill titles may be purchased in bulk for educational, business, fund-raising, or sales promotional use. For information, please e-mail SpecialMarkets@ ThomasNelson.com.

Library of Congress Cataloging-in-Publication Data

Library of Congress Control Number: 2018954527

ISBN 978-1-595557742 (Paperback)
ISBN 978-1-595557797 (Hardbound)
ISBN 978-1-595557636 (eBook)

This book is dedicated to my beloved wife Marilyn.
Her continued encouragement and prayer
brought these words to life and fruition.
I am forever blessed for our love and friendship.
I'm in love with you!

Your,
Paul Andrew Asmuth

Paul and Marilyn in 1998 at the finish of the twentieth anniversary race
Photo courtesy of *La Traversee Internationale du Lac Memphremagog*

CONTENTS

CONTENTS

FOREWORD

P aul Asmuth has nailed it! He gives us a formula for success in marathon swimming and in life. Through his unique relationships and open water experiences, Paul recounts his successes and failures, and how these challenges both shaped and fulfilled his quest to become one of the greatest marathon swimmers of all time. You'll learn life lessons, gain valuable training tips, take a crash course in ocean and river currents, get to know world-famous coaches, and be encouraged to overcome your life challenges. Pull up a world map on your smart device and trace the steps that earned Paul an induction into the celebrated International Swimming Hall of Fame.

My honor was to have been Paul's trainer during his first Around the Island Swim, a 23-mile course around Absecon Island, otherwise known as Atlantic City, New Jersey. As Paul will share, God's hand guided him in this new direction when his hopes of competing at the 1980 Moscow Olympic Games were dashed by the U.S. boycott. He found himself in unchartered waters, and having spent summers lifeguarding and boating at the Jersey Shore, I took a keen interest in Paul and his inaugural swim. At the time, I was the University of Arkansas swim coach, and I hooked up Paul with my former Springfield College coach and mentor, Charles (Red) Silvia, who helped start Paul on a new training regimen in preparation for his first victory—the very race in which I was able to resurrect the knowledge I had gained during my rowing days as a Wildwood,

New Jersey, lifeguard. Growing up on the back bays of Jersey gave me an advantage in helping Paul navigate the back waters of Absecon Island.

Paul was as hardworking as any Olympian or national champion I have ever coached in the pool. He demonstrated the determination and grit that few sportsmen exhibit. From the very first, he overcame any fear of the deep and of the creatures beneath, endured the harrowing ordeal of swimming for eight hours straight in fluctuating temperatures and currents, and was willing to suffer the mental fatigue and excruciating physical pain that accompanies such endurance feats.

Reading Paul's story will not only enlighten you further to the world of marathon swimming, but you'll soon discover that Paul is as great a person as he was a world-class swimmer. So, dive on in and be swept away in a current of aquatic and life experiences from around the world.

—SAMUEL JAMES FREAS, EdD
OLYMPIC COACH, USA NATIONAL TEAM
COACH OF WORLD-RECORD HOLDERS AND OLYMPIC CHAMPIONS
COLLEGIATE COACH OF THE YEAR
PROFESSOR, HEALTH AND HUMAN PERFORMANCE

PREFACE

Everyone has their story as to how they have come to receive awards in their lives, or why they haven't. As a young swimmer, I was not the one anyone on the pool deck would have noticed as destined to become something special. Left to my own choices and decisions, I would have achieved very little as an athlete; after all, as an age-group swimmer my definition of a successful practice was getting kicked out of practice by the coach for misbehavior.

The story of my marathon swimming journey is how the hand of God directed me throughout my life, to put me in the right place and, more importantly, with the right coaches and teammates who would build my mind, body, and spiritual path to achieve great success, as improbable as this was in my early days. This book tells many stories of a successful athletic career, and more importantly, it recognizes those who made it all happen.

I graduated college in 1980, the year the USA Olympic boycott was announced. This gave me one option to continue my passion for swimming, and that was professional marathon swimming. Going from swimming 1,500-meter (1 mile) pool races to 20-plus-mile races in oceans, lakes, and rivers was a daunting undertaking to consider. At this precise moment, God brought into my life coaches Dr. Sam Freas and Dr. Charles "Red" Silvia, who taught me the open water skills and confidence that I needed to start winning races my very first year.

The races were much harder than I ever anticipated, and in the first race when I wasn't sure about finishing, Sam made me believe. He taught me to never give up no matter how much it hurt, and to trust in God for the outcome. Besides, I don't think he would have ever allowed me to get onto the boat, unless I was sinking.

Coach Silvia taught me how to acclimate to race in cold water like the English Channel, and Lac St. Jean, and through proper stroke technique, how to swim fast, efficiently, and injury-free for 10 hours or more.

Along the way, it would have been easy to become discouraged if I had dwelled on the performance of an individual race, or a decision by a governing body that I had no control over. My longevity and success in the sport were due to many factors—and one that always served me well was to strive to take each day just one at a time and make the most of each moment, because the one thing we get to choose in any situation is our attitude.

I also knew that when we all lined up to start a race, no one cared how I did last year or last week. We were all there to win that day, and I had already spent a lot of time visualizing just that. My goal with every race was to come to the starting line prepared to be the best Paul Asmuth I could be that day. Always bringing my utmost brought success, no matter my place at the finish line.

During our vacation in October 2017, my brother John had a health scare. My wife Marilyn and I spent time in prayer and discernment, about a commitment to writing this book, which we had been talking about for many years. Why wait any longer? Marilyn took out a pad of paper and said, "Okay, let's write down the chapters of your book." For the most part, these are the chapters I'm sharing with you now. Marilyn has walked beside me the entire journey, reading every page multiple times, offering kind guidance and love during many emotional moments of writing.

The book title, *The Sport of the Soul*, is based on the fact that unlike any other sport, marathon swimming diminishes our senses to a point of uselessness. All five of them: to hear, feel, touch, smell, and see are stripped away through constant water movement against the skin, cold, hot, dark, and debilitating fatigue. During a race I move deeply into my soul, the very essence of who I am, who God made me to be. It has been written that the soul is something that cannot be pondered by the reasoning mind, which can be reasonably compared to the sport of marathon swimming. During a race, I just stroked, breathed, prayed, and kept pushing forward.

No other sport allows the mind so much time to ponder and wander. We are completely exposed to our mind's reflections, both positive and negative. The preparation time put into training our brain in advance of these challenging moments will determine whether our thoughts are helpful or harmful—whether we succeed or fail, and sometimes live or die.

Join me on an unusual adventure, inside the mysterious and challenging sport of marathon swimming. The highs, the lows, and the unexpected may take you by surprise.

May God bless you on your journey.

LA TRAVERSEE INTERNATIONALE
DU LAC ST. JEAN
1981

"You Saved my Life"

The late July day was cold and grey, with rain falling most of the swim. Winds created white caps on the coffee-colored lake waters like a field of sheep, a condition the Quebecois refer to as "mouton." Frigid and rough waters make for a very long slog in a marathon swim. Breathing to my right I looked at my brother and guide in the small 12-foot boat, providing me direction, coaching, and nourishment over the 21 miles (32 kilometers), and knew he was cold, too, as we sloshed across Lac St. Jean.

We woke up at 3 a.m., leaving Roberval at 4:30 a.m., and the bus pulled into the small village of Peribonka at around 6 a.m., to a rowdy greeting from crowds of fans who were huddled around bonfires to stay warm. Most had partied all night and were eager to cheer the swimmers as we exited the bus. "*Bonne chance* (good luck)," they yelled, knowing many on this day would not succeed. Unlike those of us who did not live here, they knew that the ice had cleared the river and lake only two months previous, and the crowd was excited to see who would be able to meet the challenge that this day brought, and who would not.

1

The race started at 7 a.m. in the Peribonka Marina, near where the Peribonka River spills into the lake. The annual 32-kilometer *La Traversee Internationale du Lac St. Jean* (the International Crossing of Lake St. John) from Peribonka to Roberval is the most prestigious marathon swimming race in the world, and the most challenging. Cold water, river currents, choppy lake, and water so dark you can barely see your hands as they pull beneath your body, demand mental focus and determination to succeed. Many swimmers have challenged the lake and some years few have finished. She exposes the strengths and weaknesses in the athletes who attempt to cross her. Many swimmers have given one or two valiant but failed attempts, or avoided confronting her at all.

On this race morning there were twenty-one swimmers starting the race, representing seven countries. Some had many years of experience and others, including me, had completed very few marathon swimming races, as I had started the sport the previous summer. We huddled in a small room at the boat marina to stay warm while race officials, coaches, boat guides, celebrities, politicians, and the media rushed around outside, preparing for our introductions and the race start. Organized chaos.

As each of us was called out for our introductions, we were hit with the icy wind and light rain that quickly reminded us that the lake was going to be a tough challenge today. The crowds of people, now in the thousands, lined the boat docks and riverbanks, cheering enthusiastically as each of us were introduced. As they called my name, "'Paul Asmuth' (pronounced As-moot by the Quebecois) *des Etats-Unis* (from the United States)," and I waved to the crowds, I felt a deep dread about what was ahead of me.

This was my brother John's first marathon swimming race as a coach in the boat. He had tremendous experience coaching on the pool deck, and was an assistant coach of the Auburn University swim team. If he was nervous I couldn't tell, I had enough nerves for both of us. He began preparing my skin for the day ahead by rubbing anhydrous lanolin on areas of my body that could chafe during the swim—under my arms, around my neck, and groin areas. Lanolin is derived from sheep's wool and serves to protect their wool and skin from the environment. For swimmers it is a great lubricant, but does nothing to protect a swimmer from the cold. On this morning, some swimmers completely covered their bodies with the white, sticky substance, hoping this would keep them warmer and help them finish the crossing. Lanolin would not be their savior.

John Asmuth, head swim coach, Auburn University

John and I prayed before he left to get into our boat, asking God to watch over us and to help me to swim to the best of my abilities, not knowing how important these prayers would become later this day. Having won the Lac St. Jean race the prior year, we were confident in my chances for success, and also aware that the chilly air and water conditions were very different from the year before. Water this cold was far from ideal for a boy who grew up on the Gulf Coast of Florida and spent the last five years training in the warm sun of either Mission Viejo, California, or Arizona State University. Neither place is known for great cold-water training conditions in June and July.

Feeling the thrill of victory in 1980
Photo courtesy of *La Traversee Internationale du Lac St. Jean*

It was time for all of the swimmers to leave the ready room and walk out on the docks in just our suits, caps, and goggles. The wind and rain continued to remind us of what the day would be like. The crowds cheered even louder as we walked out and, when we reached the dock end, jumped into the water. Burning cold immediately hit my face like millions of little needles pricking my skin, taking my breath away. I tried to relax and breathe, hoping that the race would quickly start so that I could begin generating the heat that my shivering body needed.

The swimmers lined up holding a small rope and then heard the countdown: "*Dix, neuf, huit, sept, six, cinq, quatre, trois, deux, un, BANG.*"

The starters gun sounded. With impressive arm-and-leg splashing to get our momentum started, we began swimming 400 meters upriver against the current and away from the lake. With our swimming speed slowed by the 1 mph opposing current, the crowds were able to watch us for a good length of time at the race start. The water was so cold that I had an immediate sinus-area headache of solid pain, which through experience meant the water was near 60 degrees or slightly below. I had never completed a marathon distance in water this cold.

To avoid the starting fray, I moved to the front of the pack by swimming along the outside of the thrashing arms and legs. This part of the course was a simple, straight out-and-back line marked by 20-foot-long brown logs with smooth trunks, 2 feet in diameter, which were linked together with industrial strength steel chains. There were two sets of logs, one on the course perimeter to keep boats out of this area and the swimmers safe, and the other line of logs to mark the interior swimming course.

As we swam alongside the logs, the waves created by our swimming moved them back and forth, and I could hear the chains clanging together underwater, along with the sound of dozens of motorboat propellers as they maneuvered for position. With each breath I could see the thousands of people cheering for us along the shoreline, but not hear their voices. However, their enthusiasm for the race traditions and admiration of the swimmers are always palpable to me, and I could feel their love as they watched us attempt to cross a formidable lake. Just like the logs, we were all linked together in trying to accomplish an unbelievable feat—the swimmers, the coaches, the fans, the media, and the race organizers.

After swimming upriver for about 10 minutes, we turned and headed back toward the start line. Now we were swimming with the current and the shoreline was passing very "quickly" for a swimmer. Passing the start line area, the log-lined course stopped and we entered the open river. Ahead of us all we could see is a river filled with boats. There are security, guide, and pleasure boats, along with a few kayaks. At this point of the race, the most important thing I needed to do was find my brother and guide boat. Open water swimming has no swimming lane ropes in the lakes and rivers to help with direction, and each swimmer is completely reliant on their coach to guide them and keep them safe from other boats and floating vagrant timber logs. These large pieces of wood are left over from the lumbermen using the rivers to move their wood to the mills (the rivers in Quebec are no longer used for this purpose and timber is trucked to the mills). The sooner I could get next to my boat the straighter my course would be. My view was blocked by boats, making navigation fairly impossible.

This part of every marathon swimming race is the most dangerous for the swimmers, while their individual guide boats are maneuvering to come alongside their swimmer, and the swimmers are having a hard time seeing where to go. The small guide boats each have an outboard motor with a propeller safety cover. When all of the competitors are tightly bunched in a pack at the race beginning, the guide boats tend to bump into each other like bumper cars at the fair, and tempers can be short with everyone on heightened edge, jockeying for their swimmer's best position.

After a short while, I was able to find John and settle into a relaxed rhythm of about 80 strokes per minute. With the rough, frigid water, I kept my pace a little slower than a predictable race start, knowing that I would need more energy than normal to cross the lake.

The pace was pretty slow and I felt comfortable as we swam the 3 miles downriver to the lake. After 30 minutes I moved closer to the boat and reached up for two quick cups of fuel to "feed." The warm drinks swishing through my mouth felt good against the cold water. The drinks included glucose as the energy source, mixed with either an orange-flavored electrolyte fluid or a high-caffeine black tea, called Morning Thunder, which was about the same color as the lake.

As we approached the river mouth, James Kegley, a NCAA All-American swimmer from Indiana University and an intimidating competitor, began to increase his swimming pace and moved into the lead. James was taller with bigger muscles than me, with a wonderful laugh and smile that would light up the girls' hearts. James and I both started in marathon swimming the year before and had already raced each other several times. He was the swimmer who I was most concerned with and his move to the front of the pack could not be ignored. Letting go of my race strategy, I increased my pace to catch up to James and kept a higher stroke rate of about 84 strokes per minute. Still comfortable, but definitely using more energy. The benefit of working harder was my body was generating more heat from a higher heart rate and muscle exertion; my headache was gone and I was a little more comfortable in the cold. The negative of swimming faster was using more energy earlier in the crossing. Still 18 miles to go.

With more speed I caught up and passed James, and then kept up this pace, only slowing to feed every 20 minutes. John kept me informed on the dry erase board about my stroke rate, location of other swimmers, time until we fed again, trivia, jokes, and words of encouragement to keep my spirits up. I let him know before the race not to ask how I was feeling or tell me how far to the finish. In swimming races this long I was usually very cold, tired, hurting, or nauseous and didn't want someone asking how I was feeling. Telling me how far to the finish could be encouraging or discouraging and I only wanted to focus on the next 20 minutes, nothing more.

Marathon swimming races are typically more than 7 hours and 20-plus miles. Thinking that I have 1 mile down and only 20 miles to go can be very discouraging. I found that by focusing only on the next 20 minutes, time passed very quickly and I would lose track of how many hours I had been moving. Years after retiring from swimming, a close friend, Terry, experienced a serious stroke. He chose to receive a week of very demanding physical therapy and wasn't confident he could exercise for 8 hours a day all week. I encouraged him by sharing that he didn't need to exercise for 8 hours a day, only 20 minutes at a time. And then after the first 20 minutes, have some water, take a breather, and then exercise for another 20 minutes. It was a physically and mentally challenging week for him and he pushed through very well, just 20 minutes at a time.

Now we are more than two hours into the swim and well out into the big lake with many miles ahead of us. John tells me I have a lead of 200 meters over Kegley. Lac St. Jean is large with over 400 square miles of surface, and is fairly shallow, located about 150 miles north of Quebec City. The lake is fed by dozens of small and large rivers, including the Peribonka, Mistassini, and Ashuapmushuan Rivers, before draining into the Saguenay River, and ultimately the Saint Lawrence River. The lake completely freezes in winter and the ice is so thick the community of Roberval sets up a small village of houses for ice fishing, along with a hockey rink and ice-skating track; the final ice usually clears the lake in late spring.

With so many rivers feeding into the lake, there is little time for water to warm as it is constantly on the move and quickly travels to the exit point on the Saguenay. The relatively shallow depths often turn a calm lake into a frothy mess very quickly when any wind is present. In addition, during the crossing there are many pleasure and safety boats that want to be as close as possible to the action of the swimmers, creating even more and uneven water turbulence. Depending on wind direction, motor fumes wafting across the water surface can create breathing difficulties for the swimmers.

Between the waves and tannin-colored water, I can see nothing around me when I breathe, except my brother in the small guide boat. He is my lifeline to all that I know in this moment. I breathe, stroke, stroke, breathe, stroke, stroke, breathe, trying to remain calm and in a somewhat meditative state. With my senses of seeing, hearing, touching, and tasting shut down, I am aware of my surroundings while feeling nothing at the same time. There is just my soul now, everything within me is quiet, and I am in a battle for my life, yet unaware of the danger to come.

The Peribonka River water is usually 2 to 4 degrees colder than the lake water, and I was looking forward to the water temperature rising some. On this day, with no sun and the wind churning the deeper, colder water together with the warmer upper layers, the water remains cold, and despite my energy output, I begin to shiver after only 3 hours. A sign that my body is in the early stage of hypothermia. Muscle shivering is a natural defense of the body trying to warm up as the core temperature drops. With 5 hours to go this is not a good sign. John tells me I am about 300 to 400 meters in the lead, which is positive news.

The wind and rain continue, and John has a harder time writing messages on the dry erase board and eventually has to give up. There is no more "dry" available today. John then has to start communicating with me using hand signals and quick verbal messages during our 20-minute feed breaks. Holding out both hands, fingers spread wide to indicate "10 minutes to feeding," then one hand with fingers splayed "5 minutes to feeding," I see his lips moving but hear no sound.

As we proceed farther from the north shore of Lac St. Jean and enter the center of the lake, we can see no shore, only angry brown water foaming with white caps and cloudy grey skies dumping rain. John relies on our expert boat guide to know the course and direction using his compass and transistor radio. The radio is used to follow the strongest AM frequency signal coming from Roberval and is a reliable navigational tool.

For many years, most of the boat guides have been First Nation descendants who have grown up on the lake in a reserve referred to as Pointe-Bleue (the reserve is now known as Mashteuiatsh, meaning "where there is a point"). Their experience and knowledge of the river currents, race course, and weather are invaluable to the swimmers and coaches.

My body continues to shiver and the goose bumps on my shaved legs are like sandpaper on my skin as my legs rub together, creating a grapefruit-sized road rash on the back of my left calf. I look forward to each feeding of warm liquid and keep pressing forward against the most extreme swimming conditions I have ever encountered.

A regret often propels new determination. My poor result in the previous summer when I competed in *Les Quatorze Milles de Paspebiac* (the 14 miles of Paspebiac), a marathon swimming race on the eastern coast of Quebec from Grand Anse, New Brunswick, to Paspebiac, Quebec, across the Baie-des-Chaleurs (Bay of Warmth) fueled a new attitude for me today. The bay's name must be an oxymoron, as there is nothing warm about this open water race location. The water on race day was rough and cold with fog blowing across the water so thick you could only see about 200 meters (600 feet). The guide boats were big fishing trawlers to handle the tough sea conditions of open ocean.

As the story of naming the bay is told, when Ponce de Leon was exploring this coastal area, he spent time around the mouth of the St. Lawrence River where the summer water temperatures are 45 degrees. When they headed south around the Gaspésie Peninsula and entered the Baie-des-Chaleurs, the waters were a balmy 55 degrees, so they called this the Bay of Warmth. Ha! I doubt they were swimming in the water more than 5 minutes.

After about two hours of swimming in these terrible conditions, I got out onto my boat and headed back to shore, and I was winning the race at the time. James Kegley got out of the race shortly after me. In my mind I was sure that no one would be able to finish in these sea conditions, and I certainly wasn't mentally or physically ready to take on such a challenge. I went back to my motel, had pizza for lunch, took a nap, and waited to hear how the other swimmers fared, assuming that they were all going to be out at some point in the day.

There was a knock on my door about 5 hours after I had gotten out to let me know to come down to the harbor, and watch the swimmers finish. I was completely shocked! How could anyone still be swimming in these conditions after 7 hours?

Down at the beach all I saw was the same fog from the morning blowing across the bay, and no boats or swimmers. Within 15 minutes I was able to start making out the images of some fishing trawlers about 400 meters offshore as they approached, slowly rolling side to side in the swells. They looked like a fleet of ghost ships slowly coming to shore. In another 10 minutes I could clearly see the boats with swimmers next to them. They were swimming sluggishly but still moving; it was unbelievable to me and I was embarrassed to have given up so easily in the morning without truly challenging the conditions—a deep feeling of regret that I wouldn't forget.

As I watched a handful of swimmers finish and exit the water with their swollen faces blue-grey and bodies shivering, I vowed to never give up again on a marathon swim. These competitors were true heroes, and had completed a feat that so few in the world could ever do. Claudio Plit from Argentina, Bill Heitz from Montana and an Indiana University NCAA All-American, Nassar Shazly from Egypt—amazing gladiators and experienced marathon racers. Remembering this feeling of regret on the Paspebiac beach and the mind-set of never quitting on a swim was with me today; the night before I let John know that *even if I was really tired, not to let me get out, and just encourage me to keep going.* Now, I was facing the toughest conditions I had ever experienced.

Around the five-hour time John let me know that my lead was 500 meters and that I was looking good. Little did he know how truly cold my body was as my core temperature continued to drop and my shivering increased.

Over the next two hours, hypothermia began to take more and more control of my body and mind. Despite my best efforts, my brain was getting cold, and my motor function could not operate efficiently as my core body temperature plummeted. At 7 hours, I still had a lead but was watching my lead dramatically shrink as John kept me abreast of the rest of the field; the other swimmers were catching up to me—400, 300, 200, 100 meters now, barely in front of the lead swimmers. They had caught up to me. *What was happening?*

The next two hours of swimming are a bit fuzzy to me as hypothermia began to shut down my cognitive function, and at around 8 hours my brother started speaking a foreign language, which was odd as he knew no other languages. What I did know was I couldn't understand a word that he was telling me or writing to me, and could only mutter, "What?" as I tried to comprehend his directions to me. Frustrated and confused by "John's" inability to communicate clearly, which was actually due to my semiconscious state at this point, I put my face down and kept swimming. At least I thought I was swimming, when in reality my arms were moving, but forward momentum had virtually stopped.

11

The next thing I remember was John letting the boat get too close to me, and I had to push the boat away in order to keep swimming. I learned later that John was trying to grab me, as he now understood that I was in big trouble from hypothermia.

John took charge and brought the security boat over to create a "V" with the two boats blocking my path in order to grab me, just as I lost consciousness after almost 9 hours of swimming. The finish was clearly in view to John, only 1,000 meters away (about 12 minutes of swimming on a normal day). But today the lake had defeated me.

I have no clear memories of the short boat trip to shore and quick ambulance ride to the hospital. John and the men who pulled me from the water had to be so scared. To lift an unconscious 175-pound man from the water had to be extremely difficult. They will forever be my heroes for saving my life that day, and angels watched over me, too. I do remember feeling the shaking arms of the men carrying me along the dock to the ambulance. Shaking either caused by carrying a motionless weight or their own shock and concern over how I looked.

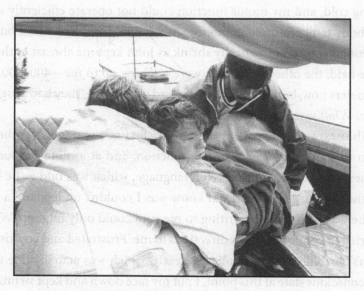

Being carried from the boat at the finish in hypothermic state;
feeling the agony of defeat
Photo courtesy of *La Traversee Internationale du Lac St. Jean*

The good news in this region is that the Roberval Hospital is used to seeing and treating hypothermic patients. There are many more cases in the winter than in July, but their care of me was the best. I don't remember much of my time at the hospital other than they put me in a warm bath for what seemed like about 20 minutes. When I mentioned the short bath to John he laughed and let me know that I was in the bathwater for 2 hours, as they slowly raised my core body temperature.

Talking about the swim later, John told me, "I had been trying to get you out of the water much sooner, but you wouldn't let the rescue craft anywhere near." He added, "And then you couldn't understand the messages I was writing to you on the board. Then you started stopping to tread water. You never asked to come out of the water, but I soon realized that you were in trouble and weren't going to make it to the finish line, which wasn't very far away. I had never experienced something like this before, and I was very scared for you."

I had no idea.

Sometimes having a mind-set that is rational when not under hypothermic conditions, i.e., "I will never get out of a race again without giving everything I have," can become lethal in the wrong rough-and-cold water conditions, especially when hypothermia is involved and the person making this decision has no cognitive function anymore. Thankfully John took charge and saved my life. Later, he had to make another tough call, to our parents. Sadly, there have been too many hypothermia deaths in marathon swims, especially at the English Channel. Even with increased knowledge of safety and craft, the drive of an athlete's mind to succeed in a crossing gets skewed under the influences of hypothermia. In these crucial moments it takes a knowledgeable support team to call an end for that day. Often against the swimmer's wishes. For me, I was very close to a hospital and could recover within hours; in the middle of the English Channel, many hours away from facilities to warm the athlete, the swimmer lays on the deck of a fishing trawler used as an escort boat, and gets colder, and heartbreakingly, lives have been lost.

On this day, only eight of the twenty-one swimmers who started the race were able to conquer the lake, with Claudio Plit winning in 9 hours, 46 minutes. Over two hours slower than my winning time the summer before. Now I wasn't sure if I ever wanted to challenge her again. In fact, I wasn't sure if I wanted to even compete in this sport anymore. I had a lot to consider and pray about, as I had almost died. *Was this the sport for me? Could I really compete in rough, cold-water races? Should I only focus on the warmer races like some of the other athletes, or truly embrace this extreme sport? Was God trying to tell me something?*

Due to the clear thinking and swift action by John and the safety team, I didn't die in Lac St. Jean, but came very close; I thanked God for watching over us, and asked him to guide me as we prepared to travel eastward to Paspebiac, for another cold-water challenge the next weekend, attempting to cross the Baie-des-Chaleurs. Was I up to it? I wasn't sure.

COACH VIRGINIA DUENKEL

Olympic Gold Medalist

The swim team in Fort Myers, Florida, had always been a summer league team. We started practicing when the weather warmed up the pool water; a heater wasn't affordable. For most of the swimmers on the Fort Myers Swimming Association team, swimming was a good break from the summer heat and gave our mothers a short respite from us. The highlights were the swim meets where there would be lots of sweets that were justified to "give us energy" for the races that were mostly 25- and 50-yard events and less than a minute long.

Like many second-born children, I did whatever my older brother John did. When he joined the swim team, so did I. I was seven years old and he was nine; neither of us had ever been on a swim team. I knew how to swim from lessons; pools were for having fun not working out. What's a "practice"?

The first day at practice was a rough one as the coach told us to swim 500 yards. "What's that?" I asked a kid next to me.

He replied, "Twenty lengths of the pool."

He might as well have said 100 lengths because that was more than I had ever swum in my whole life. To my amazement everyone jumped in and started swimming twenty laps, so I did, too. The first couple of lengths weren't too bad but then exhaustion hit; I had never done something so hard.

After about six pool lengths complete fatigue set in. Everyone was swimming past me, and I stuck my head in the corner of the pool and cried. Tears of embarrassment, fear, and anger all came gushing out. The coach was kind and let me out for a while to rest, which was even more embarrassing as I watched kids my age complete the 500 yards.

There was no quitting the team as the dues had already been paid for the summer and John was going, which meant I had to go, too. My swim team goals now became either hiding from mom when she called us to go to the pool or misbehaving so badly at practice that the coach would make me take a time out on the bench. My new definitions of success were achieved on many days.

As it turned out there were three other boys my age who happened to be really good. Clay Parnell and David McCagg were both age-group state champions in their events, Charlie Williams top five in his, and then there was me: "the hack." This must have been quite a dilemma for the coach, to have three great swimmers and the only option for the four-person relay was me. Ha!

Clay Parnell, David McCagg, Paul, Lee Anne Williams, Charlie Williams
Photo courtesy of *The Fort Myers News-Press*

For the next five summers, the four of us swam numerous relays together, winning many state championships and setting records. If there would have been a fourth swimmer anywhere near the caliber of the fast three, these records would probably stand today. On our medley relay, David would swim backstroke, Charlie breaststroke, Clay butterfly, and me freestyle, which was the only stroke I knew. By the time it was my turn to swim, we would have such a huge lead, all I had to do was finish one or two lengths of the pool, and I would go home with first place ribbons and trophies. When Clay or David weren't available, one of my best friends, Richard Johnston, who was a great backstroker, would fill in and lead us off to fast starts. The relay winning was fun and kept me in the pool swimming each summer. Winning is always fun. If it hadn't been for David, Clay, Richard, and Charlie I would have quit long before.

My lack of swimming enthusiasm continued over these five years, and the summer I turned twelve we decided not to be part of the team. Our family took an extended vacation and it didn't make sense to pay the dues for only part of the summer. My parents didn't get any complaints from me.

In the spring of 1970, we decided to be on the swim team again and practice started like every other year, except we had a new coach, Virginia "Ginny" Duenkel. She was young, tall, lean, pretty, and tan, with a big smile and even bigger laugh, who also happened to be an Olympic gold medalist from the 1964 Tokyo Olympics when she was only 16 years old, and had set multiple world records. *What?! An Olympic gold medalist on our deck? This was a serious coach.* Not only was I in complete awe of our new coach now standing on the pool deck telling us what to do, but had a big crush on her, along with all the other guys on the team. Ginny brought a serious training regime to our team that we had never known.

Our pool was only 3 feet deep on both ends and we had a bad habit of "walking our turns," which was walking on the pool bottom to shorten the turn and rest a little, instead of doing a flip turn with a hard push off. After a short period of time, Ginny let us know that this was no longer acceptable at practice, and any time we walked a turn, or stood on the bottom, we had to start over the set. Everyone had to start over.

Typical swimming workouts are broken down into mostly short distances of varying strokes and rest intervals. These snippets of the swimming workouts are known as "sets." With Ginny, our sets were now designed similar to an Olympic swimmer's preparations, and had a purpose to each workout, and each workout fit within the weekly plan. We knew our new coach was serious about the training when one day doing a set of 3 × 1,000 yards (40 laps), someone (*could have been me, probably was*) walked a turn. Ginny promptly and calmly stopped everyone in the pool with a loud whistle and, with strong resolve, let us know that someone had walked a turn, and all of us were starting over the set of 1,000s. (*Gulp, nothing like pressure from your teammates to stop bad habits, which affected everyone in the workout.*)

Not only was this a very difficult set for any of us to complete, but now we had to start over because we hadn't followed her directions for correct training. Wow! She was really passionate about proper form during workouts, and there was also now peer pressure to train right, which developed a new "team" atmosphere. With this new purpose, we all started working harder together to achieve goals we never thought possible, and to make Ginny proud.

This same season, a new swimmer my age joined the team. His name was Jeff Evans. Jeff was the state record holder in my best events, the 400- and 1,500-meter freestyles. My whole swimming world had been rocked. Workouts were very hard and tough, and there was absolutely no messing around if you wanted to be on the team. And now each workout I was crushed by the best distance freestyler in the state. There was no more showing off, or goofing around. I could either embrace these changes as challenges and opportunities or quit. I became engaged and started training hard for the first time in my life. Staring me in the face every practice was the realization that I had a long way to go to be competitive. In fact, "reality" was leading my lane and had a name: Jeff Evans.

During the years that Ginny coached the team, money was raised and a pool heater and covers were purchased and installed. We were no longer just a summer league team, and now trained year-round.

During these two years, Ginny taught me a lot about training, hard work, and achieving goals that I would have never thought achievable. One of the most important stroke lessons that she insisted we learn was to bilaterally breathe. Bilateral breathing means to breathe equally on the left and right sides of the body while swimming freestyle. Within the rhythm of moving your arms forward, this means to take a breath every 3 strokes, i.e., take a breath on the right and then stroke right arm, stroke left arm, stroke right arm, breathe on the left, stroke left arm, stroke right arm, stroke left arm, breathe on the right, and so on. What I didn't realize as I struggled with this new swimming technique was that ten years later, bilateral breathing would be one of the most important skills I could have ever learned for open water racing. What a gift I had just received.

Ginny Duenkel was an angel sent to help me get ready for competitions so much bigger than I could ever imagine. I just didn't know it yet.

Ginny Duenkel Fuldener lives in Monett, Missouri and continued coaching until just recently. She continues to compete in pool and open water swimming competitions.

Photo courtesy of Ginny Duenkel Fuldener

AROUND THE ISLAND SWIM
1980

Atlantic City, New Jersey

*"There are many things that are essential to arriving at true peace of
mind, and one of the most important is faith, which cannot be acquired
without prayer."*

—Coach John Wooden

The fear of sharks or other unseen sea creatures is one of the biggest
trepidations of people swimming in the open ocean. Swimming in
murky or turbid seas is a very spooky experience. After all, you never
really know what is down there and how big or hungry they may be.

My very first marathon swim was in Atlantic City, New Jersey, in a
race known as the Around the Island Swim. The course is approximately
23 miles circumventing Absecon Island, which contains the beach communities of Atlantic City, Ventnor, Margate, and Longport. On the north
end of the island is the Absecon Inlet and on the south end the Great Egg
Harbor Inlet. The swim had a long history, being held from 1954 to 1964
and then revived in 1979. The greatest open water swimmers in the world
had all raced here in the 1950s and 1960s.

When the 1980 Olympic boycott was announced at the USA

Swimming national championships that spring, I was crushed and lost on what to do. The swimming community as well as all Olympic sport athletes had just dedicated four years of their lives to an opportunity that was now gone. I had completely devoted myself to making the 1980 Olympic swim team, and now, although swimming the best times of my life, these hopes were dashed.

I loved swimming and everything about the process of training, traveling, friendship, and racing, and now, having just completed university, did this mean that I needed to forget my passion and start to work? As an accountant? The last career path in which I ever imagined myself. Wow! Reality set in and what a bummer.

Before completely giving up on my swimming, I remembered reading with interest an article in *Swimming World* magazine about the sport of professional marathon swimming. These were swimming races of more than 20 miles in places like Argentina, Egypt, Quebec, and Italy in lakes, rivers, oceans, and seas; plus there was prize money. I had no experience in open water swimming but knew from my training the longer the distance the better I was.

Some days coaches would ask the distance group to do a straight swim for time of 10,000 or 5,000 meters (6.2 or 3.1 miles) in the pool. I loved these days and found that I was able to maintain a very good speed for the whole distance while other swimmers found these long distances more challenging than shorter swimming sets. Maybe my stroke and ectomorphic (tall and lean) body type helped me more than others, or more likely my attitude in approaching the challenge, brought me a better performance. Whatever it was, I could swim long distances at a fast pace.

With these open water competitions in mind, I approached Sid Cassidy, a former North Carolina State distance swimmer who I read had swum and placed second in the Atlantic City marathon race the summer before. Sid gave me some brief information and I was able to contact the race organizer, Bob Frolow, as well as a former marathon swimmer, Jim Whelan, and the invitation to compete was sent.

Also at the spring USA Swimming national championships was

Coach James "Doc" Councilman, the head swim coach for Indiana University. He had coached the open water great John Kinsella, as well as the legendary Mark Spitz. Doc (as everyone called him) encouraged me to try the sport and let me know that I would need to gain a lot of weight; I was currently 6'1", and 148 pounds, with 6 percent body fat.

At Doc's recommendation I set out to gain the weight that he recommended for my first marathon swim. Eating has always been a strong suit of mine, and so extra ice cream along with enjoying peanut butter and jelly sandwiches before bedtime was no problem. Six weeks later I walked onto the pool deck of the Mission Viejo Nadadores in California for summer training, weighing a pudgy 183 pounds and had to endure the laughter of my teammates. The 35 new pounds of weight that I had gained in a short period of time made me much slower in the water, and I looked like the Pillsbury Dough Boy walking around in a Speedo swimsuit with a puffy face and dark circles under my eyes. I would have laughed at me, too. Geez, this marathon swimming gig wasn't feeling so good.

Thankfully a blessing occurred a few weeks before the Atlantic City event for which I was training. While swimming a long set in the pool one afternoon, a coach visiting for a swim meet approached and asked me what I was doing. His name was Dr. Sam Freas, and he was the head swim coach at the University of Arkansas.

Sam had seen me swim at the most recent NCAA championships, where I placed fourth in the 1,650-yard freestyle. He was interested in hearing about my training plan to swim a 23-mile marathon swimming race, and I was interested to learn that he had grown up summer lifeguarding just south of Atlantic City in Wildwood, New Jersey, where his family had a summer home. When I was done speaking about my training and weight gain, he said there was someone I needed to talk to and asked me to come with him to the pay phone on the wall outside the men's locker room.

In short order, Sam had Coach Charles "Red" Silvia on the phone from Springfield, Massachusetts. Coach Silvia had recently retired from coaching at Springfield College, where over the years he had 200

All-American swimmers, an Olympic gold medalist, and swimmers who set fourteen world records. At the time, I had no idea of the level of coach with whom I was speaking. Coach and I hit it off immediately and he was eager to hear what I was planning to do. He had also seen me swim at the most recent NCAA championships, which were held not far from his home at Harvard University, in Cambridge, Massachusetts. He was alarmed to learn that I had recently gained 35 pounds and told me to start losing weight immediately so that I felt better and could start swimming faster again. This began a very long and valuable relationship with Sam and Coach Silvia in my marathon swimming education.

What an incredible blessing that Sam and Coach Silvia came into my life at a time when I had no clue as to what I was getting into; looking back, it is so clear to see the hand of God gently guiding the way for me. Initially, there was no peace as I was setting out to try something I knew so little about and would be much harder than I could have ever anticipated. I was nervous about the future, disappointed in my weight and conditioning, and felt like I was alone in my quest. I was also still grieving the dream of making the Olympics and unsure about becoming a professional athlete, never again eligible to race in pool competitions. Was I making a mistake?

Thankfully Sam agreed to be my trainer in Atlantic City and Coach Silvia patiently guided me in my preparation and answered my hundreds of questions. How often do we drink? How much to drink? What should I drink? Should I shave my body down like a pool race? And on and on.

Giving up the late-night meals before bed my weight dropped 10 pounds to 173 pounds, and I was feeling better in workouts but still considerably slower than three months earlier. At Coach Silvia's recommendation, I started swimming open water training sessions twice a week of about 2 hours (6 miles) each session. This training was remarkably harder than any pool training I had ever done and required more recovery afterward. I had to hold my body in one position for extended periods of time, and there were no walls to push off where my body could rest every 30 seconds for a half second. Also, learning to swim straight was super important and a new skill I needed to learn, and there were no muscle breaks or pace clocks or lane lines on the pool bottom to follow. My senses were shut down, not being able to see, hear, feel, taste, or smell. Everything was so different than the pool and I was very alone, but not lonely. I could feel "me" more, the sense of my soul. Who God made me to be. And there was a new peace I was beginning to feel while swimming.

Coach Mark Schubert was the Mission Viejo coach, and I had been training with him for many years. I first started swimming with Mark in 1976; he was the toughest coach I have ever known. Mission Viejo was the distance-freestyle capital of the world, and swimmers from around the globe came to train with our team. Mark's tough training regime is legendary and there were very few people who ever outtrained the Nadadores. Our workouts were typically 2½ hours of swimming in the morning, from 5:30 to 8 a.m. Afternoon workouts started at 3:30 in the weight room for an hour and then in the pool for another 2½ hours. At the peak of our training we trained six days a week, twice a day, 5 hours in the water, and 1 hour in the weight room. Any missed workouts were made up on Sunday. I never missed workouts to make sure I had Sunday off to recover. Very tough conditioning that would ultimately pay off for me.

Mark and I had become friends over the years and he helped me after college to find a job at the Lake Mission Viejo snack shop, cooking French fries and stocking candy machines. A hot, greasy, fast-food snack shop; not a great job with my shiny, new college degree in accounting, but it gave me walking around money to pay room rent, food, and gas. Most importantly, at this time Mark was able to get me access into Lake Mission Viejo for early morning open water training swims.

This was a great lake for me to begin my open water training swims. The man-made lake waters were clear, calm, and clean with no pleasure boats. The lake was about a mile long, which gave me a good distance to time myself. I would go out with a lake lifeguard at dawn as they motored the small Boston Whaler around the lake perimeter for their morning safety check. After a few weeks of these open water workouts, I began to feel comfortable in the lake and could feel my speed, strength, and navigation skills improving.

Money through college was always tight as it was hard to train, study, travel to swim meets, and still have time for a part-time job. When it came time to buy airfare to Atlantic City, Mark loaned me the funds, not knowing if I would finish the race or not. I didn't know, either.

Sam met me when I arrived in Philadelphia and we drove to his family's home on the back bay of Wildwood, where I met his wife, Rosemary, and his parents. They provided a comfortable place to sleep, the air was sticky hot, and fortunately I was used to the warm, humid weather from growing up in Florida.

The next day Sam and I drove to Atlantic City to go over the course. We rented a boat and checked out some of the key strategic race locations that we would need to navigate through. There would be a lot of current, which I would need to swim with and against during the race, and it was crucial to know our course strategy at each position in advance.

After seeing most of the course, Sam told me to swim in the water at the south end of the island in the Longport inlet. The tide was rushing out and he had me swim directly into the current. After an hour of swimming against the current I was pretty tired and had covered about 100 meters instead of 3 miles. Clearly this was not a good race strategy, but Sam wanted me to feel what it was like when the current was pushing against me and avoid this whenever possible.

As we pulled back into the marina, there was a 7- or 8-foot mako shark hanging from the big fishhook at the dock.

"Wow, that is a big shark," Sam yelled. "Where'd you catch it?"

The fisherman yelled back, "Only about a mile out from shore. The bluefish are running near shore right now and the makos are following the schools."

WHAT?! Alarm bells were going off in my head and I was crazy worried now about the swim, as we would be at least ½ mile offshore at the midpoint of the ocean leg. Definitely close to where the shark was caught. In addition, these ocean waters have very limited visibility due to surf, sand, and back bay runoff. *Unbelievable.* I was visibly shaken. Definitely not a pool race.

Sam, being ever the optimist, said, "Don't worry, my dad has a shotgun that I will bring in the boat with me, and if I see a big shark I'll shoot it." Wow, this was a comforting thought: Sam trying to keep his balance while standing up in a moving lifeguard dory rowing through ocean swells, aiming to shoot a large shark that was coming swiftly toward me. Yep, just like Elmer Fudd on Bugs Bunny hunting rabbits. "No problem, piece of cake," I said to myself. The power of prayer has much better odds.

Then I read in the paper that large schools of bluefish have been known to attack swimmers. "Really great, really great," I muttered to myself. *What had I gotten myself into?* Completing the swim was now only one of my worries and there was no turning back. I needed to repay Mark the airfare if I could; his odds of repayment were going down.

The race organizers couldn't have been nicer to Sam and me as we met with them and the swimmers during the days before the race, at meetings and social events. The competitors and their coaches were mostly from foreign countries, and it was a very interesting group of eighteen men and nine women from six countries. The stories from other races and places around the world were fascinating. There was a race from Capri to Naples, Italy, in the Mediterranean Sea and another one that sounded crazy, down the Rio Coronda River in Argentina, where you were swimming with the current for 8 hours, covering more than 50 miles. *Swimming World* magazine had a picture showing thousands of people on a bridge, watching the Rio Coronda race that I had seen and was inspired by. What a remarkable and eclectic group of athletes; it was my first truly international race and everything was so new and unique to my swimming and life experiences.

Over the next couple of days while in Atlantic City, we took advantage to swim at key strategic race points, especially the inlets. Sam also introduced me to the famous White House sub shop so I could have my first Philly Cheesesteak; it was delicious. Besides these short training sessions, I rested and limited my activities before the Saturday race; it was good to be staying in a quiet Wildwood neighborhood. At this time, Atlantic City was building many new casinos and a hub of bustling activity created lots of traffic congestion.

The night before the race I shaved my arms, legs, and torso just like I would for any pool competition. Shaving off body hair helps to streamline the body, reducing drag, increasing efficiency, and stimulates the nerve endings, which creates a new "feel" for the water, just like the smooth skin of a bottlenose dolphin (I wish I could swim as fast as these amazing sea mammals). Men with a lot of body hair have very significant increases in their speed when shaved down. For me this was just a normal process of getting ready for an important race and I figured everyone would be shaved down on race morning, just like championship pool competitions.

Thinking about the challenges of the next day I didn't sleep much the night before the race. Sam and I were up very early, making our race drinks, a combination of electrolytes and glucose. Neither of us had done this before so we were learning as we prepared and relied a lot on Coach Silvia's advice.

We loaded up the car with everything that we thought we would need for the race: binoculars, 1 foot × 2-foot course map Sam shellacked onto wood, compass for ocean leg, extra caps and goggles, cups, drinks, outboard motor grease for chafing, dry erase board, towels, and one shotgun. I had never been so nervous before a race. My mouth was dry and my heart was beating faster than normal. I was very quiet and about to learn if I could take on this challenge.

Based on Coach Silvia's recommendation, our drinks consisted of Polycose (a glucose polymer that was easily digestible and quickly absorbed), mixed with an electrolyte powder, Carboplex, for carbohydrates, and Coca-Cola. Everything was chilled for the warm water in the back bay.

The race started at 8:15 a.m., and driving through downtown Atlantic City at 6 in the morning was a unique experience. The only people out and about were the gamblers just coming out of the casinos and the ladies of the night walking the streets. What a dichotomy of events going on at the same time with athletes lining up to start a marathon swimming race while the rest of the town was just finishing their marathon race of a hard life, a life much tougher than what the swimmers were about to endure.

Arriving at the historic Gardner's Basin Marina, there was a buzz of activity with each swimmer having a lifeguard dory needing to be launched into the water, two lifeguard rowers, their coach and equipment, safety boats, and hundreds of spectators. There was a lot going on! The race director was yelling at the lifeguards to get their boats in the water and ready as there was pressure to start the race on time due to the tidal influences of the race. Starting 15 minutes late could add an hour to the swim for some athletes.

Sam and I were introduced to the Atlantic City lifeguards who would be rowing for us that day. Each New Jersey shore beach town from Atlantic City to Cape May sent lifeguards and boats for the competition. The race was a marathon row for the guards and they had better be in shape for a day typically lasting more than 8 hours, or they would end up hurting more than the swimmers. The lifeguards were serious athletes, too, and took great pride in helping the swimmers and coaches.

One of our rowers for the day was a beach sergeant who had been working the shore for many years and knew the waters well. The other rower was much younger and strong-looking, which was pleasing to Sam. Unfortunately, the boat assigned to us was an older wooden dory and much heavier than the newer fiberglass boats. It was a tough boat draw for our rowers who had taken a fairly slow swimmer around the year before; they had no concept of how fast I swam. Between the old heavy boat and my swimming speed, they were in for a rough day and this was worrying Sam.

The morning was a typical July New Jersey shore morning, with temperatures around 70 degrees and light winds off the ocean. There were a lot of boat fumes wafting around from the Coast Guards' diesel engines to the small outboard motors, which reminded me of my days boating in Florida (getting up early to go waterskiing sounded a lot better right now). The early morning sun looked like a giant orange ball coming through the humid haze that was sitting over the ocean.

While the ocean temperature would be temperate, around 70 degrees, portions of the back bay would be very warm, with temperatures above 80 degrees, and by late afternoon the heat levels could reach 90 degrees or more, with smothering humidity. The boys in the boat would suffer in the heat and we all needed to stay well hydrated and avoid overheating.

Race Director Bob Frolow is on the bullhorn, yelling for everyone to get into their boats. The coaches are getting their swimmers ready and Sam rubs the blue outboard motor grease around my neck and under my arms. We figured that if we used a waterproof grease that was made to hold up in extreme saltwater conditions, this would most likely offer the best lubrication. We were right, but it may not have been that healthy of a product to rub on my skin. No one else had blue grease on and they must have thought we were nuts (they were right) as they rubbed on either Vaseline that quickly wears off in warm salt water or lanolin that would stay on a lot longer than petroleum jelly.

I noticed that none of the other swimmers had shaved their bodies and thought this to be odd. Maybe they thought that I was the one who didn't know what he was doing, which was true.

Before getting into our lifeguard dory, Sam and I prayed for safety for us and the other participants, and that God would give me the strength I needed to finish the race. Boy, would I need His Divine strength today, both physically and mentally. I was really scared and once again wondered what I had gotten myself into, and wasn't ready for Sam to leave. Sam had to go and got onto the back of the boat, and cast off with the other coaches and rowers while all of the swimmers jumped into the water. Was I crazy to be doing this? I hoped not. But now I was waiting for the starter's pistol to sound and begin a 23-mile race. I had never raced more than 1 mile and that was in a pool; no turning back now.

The race starter gave us a 2-minute notice and I swam around the marina, loosening up and trying to stay calm, then a 1 minute notice and I grabbed the rope with the other swimmers. The rope was an old boat line with small, orange crab pot floats attached so it didn't sink, and was extended between the shore and a boat designating the starting line. With everyone holding the rope it quickly sank under the water, but we were all essentially in a straight line. I was wondering if the start really mattered much anyway; after all, we were going to be swimming for 8 hours.

There was a very old, black merchant sailing ship on our side of the marina, and I could see the US Coast Guard station on the opposite side of the docks and was pleased to know the Coast Guard would be out on the water with us. Maybe they had guns, too.

The starter pistol sounded and everyone took off like they were swimming a 100-meter race. I thought, *What is going on?* Because if this was the race pace I was in big trouble. I quickly learned that the rush was to get behind their dory and start drafting the boat. Swimming behind a rowboat or swimming close enough to feel the pull of the water already moving forward is called "drafting" and a huge advantage in open water racing. By swimming close enough to another competitor's feet, the following swimmer can go just as fast as the lead swimmer with as much as 25 percent less energy. Drafting behind the dory allowed the swimmers to push as hard as they could and go much faster than if they were swimming by themselves. So the sooner a swimmer could get behind their boat and start drafting, the faster they would go. The boat also broke through the waves and offered smoother water for increasing speed.

Each competitor's boat had a large flag of their country waving from the bow. It was a beautiful sight to see all of the dories with colored flags flying, along with safety and pleasure boats headed out to sea in the early morning light. As we were swimming out into the ocean, the coastline was lined with hundreds of fans walking or riding bicycles along the board-walk as we gradually made our way along the rocky shore and jetties.

Start of the Around the Island Swim, Atlantic City, New Jersey
Photo courtesy of James Kegley, James Kegley Photography, www.jameskegley.com

I was trying hard to get the hang of drafting behind a boat for the first time. I couldn't see the transom well under the water and I kept lifting my head to get the right spacing. Wow, staying in the draft was hard; the boat was moving side to side with the swells, we were all learning our timing together, which was key, and if I kept lifting my head all day this was going to slow me down by forcing my hips lower and create a lot of lower back and neck pain. I had to find a way to focus on the keel of the boat underwater and not lift my head so much. The rowers were also having a hard time keeping a steady pace, and I kept hitting my hands on the boat's stern when their rowing rhythm was out of sync, and that could be disastrous if I were to break a finger smashing into the transom.

Sam had a lot of experience rowing as a Wildwood lifeguard and took charge of the rowing pace by pushing the oars of the sergeant rowing in front of him. With the boat pace now going steady, I focused on a nice, smooth rhythm and stared at the bottom of the boat underwater. We were making progress.

We entered the ocean and took a 90-degree turn south. Absecon

Island is a barrier island, a little more than 7 miles long with a slight westerly concave shape. If all went well the ocean leg of the swim would take us about 2½ hours, and then we would swim 16 miles in the back bay where the narrow channels weave around and are protected from the wind, and would be calm in most places. The ocean was not calm, and we were swimming into a stiff breeze; the rowers were working hard against the waves to maintain a good speed in our heavy wooden boat.

James Kegley, a NCAA All-American distance swimmer from Indiana University, was in his first race, too. He was about 6 feet 3 inches tall, a very strong swimmer, and with a lot of swimming speed. James shot out to a strong lead in the ocean leg, and I tried to stay focused on my own pace and not get caught up in racing too soon. It would be a long day and my goal was to finish. My longest training swim had been 3 hours, and I wasn't sure how my body would hold up for 8 hours. I started to let all of the multitude of external factors fall away and just focus on my own tempo and nothing else—stroke, stroke, breathe, stroke, stroke, breathe. Finding my pace, finding me, learning what I was really made of, and I began settling into the rhythm of my soul.

Suddenly I saw a large, dark shadow pass below me from left to right that scared me to death. I looked up and yelled to Sam, "What was that?" And there he was standing up with the shotgun, just like fearless Elmer Fudd. My worst nightmare was being lived and I wanted to get onto the boat right then, but touching the boat would immediately disqualify me. Being the great coach he is, Sam assured me everything would be fine and to keep going. My adrenaline was surging like crazy. I started shaking and needed to calm down but was having a hard time with that in the moment. After 10 minutes or so, the gun was put away and Sam acted like nothing had happened. Of course, he wasn't the one in the water. Stroke, stroke, breathe, stroke, stroke, breathe... *Focus!*

Because the ocean was so rough, Sam had to keep helping to row our heavy boat so there was no communication on the dry erase board. When I stopped to drink every 20 minutes, there would be a quick burst of information: "Kegley 500 meters ahead, pick it up" or "1 mile from Longport inlet, let's make a move now" while I drank as quickly as I could, typically around 5 to 7 seconds. Then I was back to staring at the stern of the boat.

I began to feel new experiences of pain in my shoulders, elbows, neck, and lower back after about 2 hours into the race. I was hurting in places that had never bothered me before, like my elbows and lower back. Most swimmers endure some shoulder pain during their careers, but the other areas of my body were new to me. In my training swims I wasn't lifting my head to sight my course, or looking intently forward to stay near a boat to draft. These were all first-time experiences for me and my muscles and tendons were not happy. At each feed I had to start bending over underwater to stretch my lower back for a quick few seconds to loosen the muscles and relieve some pain. I knew I was losing precious distance and time by stretching, but the temporary relief was worth it.

Every now and then I would get a zap from a jellyfish sting and that would sure wake me up! The stings along my body weren't too bad, but the stings to my face felt like being pricked by a thousand little needles and slimed at the same time. What a day so far, and still 6 hours to go. I started remembering words from our Fort Myers swim team theme song: "Smilin' through the rain, laughin' at the pain"; plenty of pain to go around today. "I better keep laughin.'"

During the days before the swim, Sam and I had studied the tide charts and deciphered what we expected to happen at each critical point of the race. The inlet by Longport was key and we had practiced exactly where I would swim without following the boat; I was confident as we approached the inlet. Kegley had opened up a good lead over the other swimmers and was still a good 500 meters (about 6 minutes) ahead of me.

What I learned is that the changing of the tides from high to low creates currents as the gravity pull of the moon, sun, and earth shifts the waters back and forth across the globe. Local tides can be influenced by wind and waves, but in the end the water will still move where it has been predestined to go. While we practiced swimming in the currents at the times we expected to encounter each location, shifting sands and winds could have changed all of that from our practice runs.

There were at least 150 people on the Longport jetty boulders cheering James and me as we swam past, with many American flags being waved. It felt really amazing to be representing the USA in such a prestigious event. For the first time I realized that while I was representing the Mission Viejo Nadadores swim team, I was more importantly representing the United State of America.

James and his crew entered the inlet and were a bit farther offshore in the deeper channel, hoping to catch the incoming tide. Sam and I had planned to stay closer to shore, reasoning that the tide wouldn't be running much yet, and we started to rapidly catch them as we took the shorter distance next to the beach and rode the currents created by the shore break. I hugged the inlet beach as we had planned, swimming in very shallow water while Sam remained in deeper water so the boat wouldn't get stuck in the sandy bottom. The disadvantage of this strategy was that I wasn't drafting behind the boat, and if the tide did start running inland sooner than we anticipated, James would be in a much better position than me. This was a big risk and was definitely working to our advantage.

As I rounded the rock jetty marking the entrance to the back bay, we had made up a big margin but were still behind James. The water was now in slack tide and not moving much as we swam northerly through the community of Longport. The docks of the Longport homes were full of people cheering for us and celebrating the race with friends. Bruce Springsteen was a huge favorite in this area and "Born to Run" could be heard blasting at the parties when I stopped to feed.

After swimming under the Longport Bridge, Sam and I had decided to take another risk and swim straight through a small channel between two grassy islands. We had spoken with Ray Scott who owned the local marina and found that the water wouldn't be moving very fast when we would be navigating through. James and his crew stayed to the right in the main channel, hoping to ride a big push from the incoming currents, and we took a shorter distance straight in shallower water.

The high marsh grasses on the small island separating us from the main channel prevented us from seeing James's boat, and we had no idea if our gamble was paying off. When we exited the island channel it was clear that the risk was worth it and the lead James had over us was now cut in half—we were swimming very close to each other. I noticed James's boat was the lighter-weight fiberglass and only one rower had to work in the calmer waters. Ugh, for our crew!

In the calmer waters our rowers now had a much easier time of moving our boat and I looked up to see the beach sergeant sitting in Sam's seat, cooling off his blistered hands in the water. Sam was now rowing full time and giving this lifeguard a break; he was not in shape for this type of endurance challenge. What a blessing it was to have Sam in my boat and able to step in and row the boat fast enough to compete. Without his dory rowing skills and strength to row I would have had no chance to stay near the front with James. A true blessing.

From the race start we had swum about a mile out into the ocean, seven miles in the ocean leg, and now another 2 miles into the back bay— 10 miles or so. Crazy, we weren't even halfway done and I had now swum farther than any time in my life, sore and beyond exhausted. At least no large sea creatures or jellyfish were in the warm estuary waters.

The back bay waters began to turn from green to tannic brown and the temperature rapidly increased to more than 80 degrees. As we moved farther away from the ocean, the air heat also began to rise as the cool ocean breezes were blocked by the many homes along the shore. In the grassy areas, greenhead horse flies would bite my face when I stopped to drink. I was lucky to put my face back into the water quickly while Sam and the crew had to fight them off all day.

James and I were now trading the lead back and forth at this point, with neither of us able to sustain a big move. After more than 4 hours of swimming I knew that we were both hurting bigtime and had never experienced so much pain. My elbow tendons were screaming at each stroke, which was new to me as I had never had any elbow pain before. Both shoulders ached with every stroke and my neck muscles burned from both lifting my head and turning to breathe already thousands of times, and I knew my lower back would not stop yelling at me until the race was over. I also knew that James and the other competitors were feeling their own pain. So this was what marathon swimming was like—unbelievable. Much tougher than I could have ever imagined.

As we entered a one-mile straight channel in the town of Ventnor, Sam asked me to really push hard for the next mile, and I did. By the end of the straightaway I had opened up a 100-meter lead, and now the channel span narrowed and there were many turns where we would push harder when James's boat couldn't see us after each turn. The strategy worked and the lead began to grow.

We swam under the bridges at Dorset Avenue and then Albany Avenue, with homes lining both sides of the narrow canal. Up until this time there had not been much to see or smell and my senses had been dulled out. With the backyard BBQs blazing, there was now a lot that smelled amazing. But what was most incredible were the number of people on the bridges and docks cheering for us as we plowed our way through the bay waters.

Soon we left the homes and were in the final 5 miles of the race. There were no people, only the estuary marsh grasses around us. It was complete drudgery as I struggled through the extreme pain and deep fatigue, and I was now hot. Sam gave me some cold Coca-Cola with the fizz taken out to perk me up. A nice cold treat.

As we approached the Absecon Boulevard Bridge I began to feel the current from the incoming tide pushing against us, and I could see how hard the rowers were now working to maintain the speed of our heavy wooden boat. Sam was having to help the rowers again. Bridges are often built where the rivers or channels are the narrowest, and then large abutments are built for the bridge footings, further tightening the channel. This channel narrowing causes the currents to pick up speed underneath bridges as the same amount of water is moving through a smaller opening.

The current under the bridge was wicked and Sam started banging the back of the boat to get me to swim faster. *Bam, bam, bam!* I could hear the sound reverberate underwater. I swam as fast as I could at this point in the race day and stayed behind the boat for as long as possible until I had to get out of the deeper, faster-moving water and swim next to the shore where the current was slower. Wow, that was tough.

Making our way along the grassy islands and shoals, I had to swim right next to the shore and out of the current, which was increasing in speed as we approached the ocean inlet and Brigantine Bridge. I could feel the mushy, muddy bottom with my hands stroking through the water only about 12 inches deep. The heat was radiating off the black, mucky bottom, and the smell of sulphur from decomposing grasses was an overwhelming stench.

Mile after mile nothing but marsh grass, mud, heat, and funky odors. Then out of nowhere two fans with a big sign cheering me on. Where did they come from? There were no homes nearby. They must have walked miles to be in this spot. Sam made sure that we stopped to acknowledge them. It was a special moment and I needed the encouragement.

We could see the Brigantine Bridge, and pushing against the current it felt like *forever* to get there. Dozens of boats were now following our progress, cheering us on, and tooting their horns as we approached Gardner's Basin Marina, where we began over 7 crazy hours ago. Sam and I knew that going underneath the final bridge would be the hardest part of the day.

We had talked about where I would swim under the bridge, but not practiced. The Brigantine Bridge is supported by very large concrete columns that channel the water, creating higher-current speeds between them. The plan was for me to swim as close as possible to the shore. By now the current was at full strength, running directly against us, and I swam to the right, close to shore, away from the boat. I could see Sam and the crew struggling mightily to make any progress as the swift currents moved both me and the boat sideways. Sam and the two rowers strained with all they had. Neither the boat nor I were making progress against the current and we all pushed with whatever we had left to somehow complete the last 500 meters. It took us at least 10 minutes to go 100 meters under the bridge, and then we were through.

Life is like this sometimes, when the currents of every day are pushing us in ways we don't want to go, or rushing directly at us, holding us in place. And then at other times, life's currents push us gently forward at just the right speed, until suddenly we're moving forward so fast we are frightened. There may be a "boat" to save us, and then at other times, when we just need to trust God and push through to the finish with everything we have left, this was one of those days for me. So I kept on pushing.

Coming into Gardener's Basin was the most emotional moment of my entire swimming career. I had won a lot of pool races before but never experienced emotions like these. Joy at having won, relief for having finished and able to pay back Mark the airfare, confirmation that I had made the right choice to compete, become a "professional" athlete, and personal pride for banishing my fears of the open water challenges and distance. Tears filled my goggles and I had never felt as happy when my hand finally touched the finish line rope that we were all holding 7 hours and 36 minutes earlier. Hundreds of people cheered us from the docks and boat horns blasted, creating an amazing magical moment.

Coach Sam Freas and Paul at the end of the Around the Island Swimming race

I was still crying happy tears when I got out of the water to hug Sam; he was crying, too. Neither one of us could believe what had just happened. What an amazing feeling of joy and relief. The shoulder and elbow pain would last for more than a week, but in this moment, I felt nothing but euphoria. The lifeguards also did an amazing job rowing the marathon, and we were all exhausted.

It was pure joy and relief after winning my first professional
marathon swimming race.
Photo credit: *The Press of Atlantic City*

Media and race organizers were all buzzing around us and people were calling me "Paulie" and saying, "Way to go, Paulie" and "Yo, Paulie," like the *Rocky* movie. I didn't know people really talked like that.

James Kegley finished about 15 minutes later, and James Barry, the 1979 winner, another 20 minutes after that for third place.

Thankfully "Elmer Fudd" in the boat didn't kill any wabbits today, but Sam and I sure slew some demons of doubt. Thank you, Lord.

After getting cleaned up, James Kegley and I were approached by two men from a small town in Quebec, called La Tuque. Neither of us had ever heard of the place or their race. They wanted James and I to partner in a 24-hour, two-man relay race. *Twenty-four hours, really? In cold water, really? Any sharks?*

We were too numb and sore at the time to consider any other races and did not give them an answer.

COACH GREGG TROY

"Smilin' through the rain, Laughin' at the pain"

Coach Troy was only twenty-one years old when he took over the coaching role of the Fort Myers swim team in the fall of 1972; I had just turned fifteen. "Gregg," as he wanted us to call him, influenced my life more than any other person over my four years of high school. While Coach Ginny Duenkel taught us the fundamentals of hard work and stroke technique, Gregg taught us to work harder both physically and mentally, along with having more fun.

Coach Gregg Troy, 1978 USA Swimming National Championships,
The Woodlands, Texas

Swim practice became something that I looked forward to for the fun-loving spirit of our new coach, and also to dread for the intensity of our workouts. Country and Southern rock music blared from the boom box—Willie Nelson, Waylon Jennings, Elvis Presley, Charlie Rich, David Allen Coe, the Charlie Daniels Band, Lynyrd Skynyrd, the Allman Brothers Band, and many more. Country music was new to me, and something I learned to love and still enjoy.

We had a really tough group of young men and women who trained hard and wanted to swim fast. Many of us would go on to swim at Division I universities on NCAA scholarships and win world and NCAA championships, and become NCAA swimming All-Americans, which was unusual for such a small-town team and a credit to Gregg.

The Wes Nott pool was a small, 6-lane-by-25-yard shallow-water pool. Our lanes were crowded, and in the hot Florida summer afternoons, the water temperature was above 85 degrees. We prayed for cooling rains or times when Gregg would hose us off with cool water from the spigot. Some days were brutally hot and we pushed each other through challenging sets in the toughest of environments. Whenever the hit single "Keep on Smilin'" came on the radio, Gregg would give us a small break in practice and crank up the boom box so we could all sing the refrain "Smilin' through the rain, laughin' at the pain, rollin' with the changes till the sun comes out again." Then he would continue to crush us. At least we would have a good tune in our heads as we swam lap after lap.

Gregg opened our minds to new possibilities of success as we read together *Jonathan Livingston Seagull* by Richard Bach and discussed key quotes like:

> *"You will begin to touch heaven, Jonathan, in the moment that you touch perfect speed. And that isn't flying a thousand miles an hour, or a million, or flying at the speed of light. Because any number is a limit, and perfection doesn't have limits. Perfect speed, my son, is being there."*
>
> — Richard Bach, *Jonathan Livingston Seagull*

Our coach was not only preparing our bodies but now also our minds for success and teaching us not to limit ourselves in any way. This was transforming to me as I considered for the first time that I could be a really good swimmer.

At this time Fort Myers had three high schools: Fort Myers, North Fort Myers, and Cypress Lake. Fort Myers High School where I attended historically had the best swim team, but now my new coach was a teacher and swim coach at Cypress Lake High School, our bitter rival. This presented a problem for me emotionally as my toughest opponent, Jeff Evans, who was far more my superior in swimming, also attended Cypress Lake and would be getting extra coaching from Gregg.

Freshman year of swimming was a challenge for me as I was such a late bloomer that my nickname was "Peanut," and I was a boy swimming against men. During my sophomore year of high school, I began to train with more purpose and was experiencing the results of the hard training. The legendary Coach Wes Nott had coached the Fort Myers swim team for a long time and his workouts weren't nearly as tough as Gregg's, so I would stay and complete a second workout with Gregg and our club team after the high school team finished.

One day, between the two workouts, I decided to start practicing what it would feel like to beat Jeff Evans, who currently was much faster and stronger than I was. Most people would have laughed at the absurdity of what I was doing so I didn't share this mental training technique. I would start halfway out in the pool and sprint in the 12½ yards as fast as I could, touching the wall and then jumping and dancing around in the lane with my hands raised above my head in celebration of the imagined victory. This feeling of excitement over my anticipated accomplishment was amazing, and I repeated this over and over with goose bumps rising on my arms and legs.

After having done this for a time, Gregg saw me dancing around one day and asked me what I was doing. I replied, "I'm practicing beating Jeff Evans." He didn't laugh and just said, "Well, all right then, keep it up." Because in his mind, he had to be thinking "that may never happen" as he looked at a scrawny sixteen-year-old kid who was 5'7" tall and weighing 115 pounds. Not exactly the prototype body of an Olympic swimmer, or even a good high school one.

Gregg was slight himself and, maybe to help me feel more special, started the "Small, Wiry Guys Club." Not many on the team could be a member, as you had to be both small and wiry to get into the club, and it was a lot better than being Peanut. The requirements of the club meant that the members, while shorter than most, were also strong, lean, and sinewy. Just another thing that a great coach did to boost my confidence.

Maybe it was Gregg's mental coaching, readings of books like *Jonathan Livingston Seagull*, or I just don't have it in my DNA, but I never had any swimming idols. In fact, I really didn't pay attention to who the leaders in my events were and only focused on becoming the best Paul Asmuth that I could be. Of course, Jeff Evans was still crushing me every day in practice and swim meets, so it was hard to ignore that fact and it gave me extra motivation.

Gregg continued to push the limits of what our bodies could physically handle. Thankfully I was young and typically recovered quickly. If two workouts a day were good preparation, why not three a day? With this in mind, one summer, Gregg would meet me at the pool during my lunch breaks from the Coca-Cola bottling plant so we could train another 3,000 yards or so. Maybe it was going from the 6 a.m. 2-hour practice to the Coke plant, running back and forth from the plant to the pool along Highway 41 in the blazing Florida sun and humidity while wolfing down my lunch sandwiches, sorting empty Coke bottles in the afternoon heat, and then another 2-hour afternoon practice in a pool that was now 85-plus degrees that finally led me to reach the tipping point of fatigue. That summer both Gregg and I learned that there really could be such a thing as too much training, going fifteen or sixteen workouts in a week along with a 40-hour-a-week job. It turned out to be a bummer of a summer. I was so exhausted that during a 1,500-meter freestyle pool race I missed a flip turn at the wall so badly my feet never touched. The turn judge disqualified me; she was my best friend's mom (very hard to be disqualified swimming freestyle). I certainly wasn't touching any "perfect speed" like Jonathon Livingston Seagull. Lessons learned.

While I worked regularly with a lawn-mowing route and custodial work at my dad's church, this money all went into the savings account or ski boat gas. There was rarely any money hanging out in my pocket and the bank money was for college. Some people even told me I was "cheap." I preferred *thrifty* after my Scottish grandpa. Gregg and I started going out to lunch regularly and my hand was slow to reach for the check or my pocket for money to chip in. This is when I learned from Gregg that it was "SMBWIF"—"so much better when it's free"! And, yes, it was.

During my sophomore year of high school, there was a revival on our football field by a minister known as the Chaplain of Bourbon Street. Never having been to New Orleans I didn't have any idea of what Bourbon Street was like or anything about this young minister named Bob Harrington. But the upcoming revival was part of a lot of conversations and I decided to go see what all of the fuss was about. Since my dad was a minister I had been to many, many church services, just never a revival.

The service was in the fall at the end of the day so sitting outside wasn't too hot (no one would have come if it was in the sun). We sat on the grass field in latte-colored metal folding chairs. (This was the kind that we used to "load" by pushing up the metal seat while setting up the chairs. When a person sat down there would be a "pop" noise and my friends and I would all laugh when the *pop, pop, popping* started sounding all over the venue.)

The service started with wonderful music and Bob Harrington telling funny jokes; I loved my dad who had a great sense of humor, but there were few jokes in the Presbyterian Church services. Then he started speaking about being "saved" and "born again," and having our sins washed away by accepting Jesus into our hearts. Wow! I had never heard about this before, and felt he was speaking directly to me.

Being a preacher's kid "PK" growing up, I had spent most of my childhood trying to prove to my peers that I was no goody, goody church kid. There were many things that I had done that I wasn't proud of, and now there was a minister preaching right to me about these shortcomings and forgiveness. Near the end of the service Chaplain Bob asked us to come up to the stage if we wanted to accept Jesus into our hearts and be renewed in spirit.

Most of my life I'd spent running away from God, and now with tears rolling down my cheeks I walked toward God, right up to the stage while the choir sang the hymn "Just as I am, though tossed about, with many-a conflict, many-a doubt; fightings and fears within, without, O Lamb of God, I come, I come," and asked Jesus to come into my heart and be my Lord and Savior. My life would never be the same, and now I was swimming for someone besides myself, and knew that God loved me just as I am. No more running away, and that felt really, really good. I was redeemed.

By the time my junior year in high school started I was beginning to add muscle and fill out, but still much smaller and thinner than the other boys against whom I was racing. During this year I finally did beat Jeff Evans in a dual swim meet with Cypress Lake, and it felt as good as all of the times I had mentally and physically practiced this occasion, along with some happy tears. I knew that Gregg was really proud of me that day, too, even if I did beat his team's swimmer. Over many years together, Jeff and I stayed good friends and continued to push each other at every practice, making both of us swim faster.

By the end of my senior year in high school I had grown to 5'10", and weighed 128 pounds, still undersized for my age. But I continued to gain strength and speed from the unrelenting, challenging workouts. At the Florida state championships my times were good enough for eighth place in the finals. There were no serious NCAA Division I swimming coaches calling to offer scholarships; I still had a long way to go.

When I tried out for the swim team my freshman year at Auburn University I was a non-scholarship athlete known as a "walk on." Walk on athletes don't have much clout compared to the swimmers on scholarship and are often cut from the team, but thanks to Gregg, I was very well prepared and made the final team roster for the year. The Auburn workouts were tough, but not nearly as hard as what I had been used to, and I swam well that year for the Auburn Tigers and Coach Eddie Reese, thanks to Coach Troy.

Having a coach who is also a best friend was a great blessing to me. Gregg and I remain friends and I've always been so proud of his coaching accomplishments over many Olympics and at the University of Florida. What a treat it was to room with Gregg in Singapore while at the 2008 Beijing Olympics swim team training camp. The Olympic preparation went well and the team stayed at a hotel with wonderful culinary offerings; it was SMBWIF all the time.

Gregg challenged and inspired me to become a great swimmer and told me that if I was 6 feet tall someday, I would be a world champion. I believed him and he was right. It just happened outside the pool, in waters neither of us could have ever fathomed.

The years we trained together were the most important of my swimming years. The challenges in the pool and joys outside made swimming more special and the long journey enjoyable. Without Gregg's help and encouragement, I would not have continued to swim after high school and accomplish so much success.

EGYPT
1980

After my first successful summer of marathon swimming I was invited to Egypt for two races in September of 1980. I had never been on a transatlantic trip by myself and was intimidated by the travel and unknown experience. However, I was encouraged by Nabil Shazly and his son, Nasser (a fellow marathon swimmer), along with other Egyptian race organizers I had met over the summer that all would be well, and I booked my flights on TWA.

As we approached Cairo late at night I was amazed to see the pyramids and the Great Sphinx of Giza brilliantly lit up at night. They were beautiful and massive, dwarfing everything around them. Wow, I was looking at something built almost 5,000 years ago; this was going to be really cool and I was excited to be in Egypt!

When the plane landed in Cairo after more than 24 hours of flying from Los Angeles, most of the airport area was dark and lit with unfamiliar orange-colored lights. I was very tired and nervous, hoping that there would be someone at the airport to meet me as I only had a phone number and address of the race headquarters, which would be closed at this hour. There were very few Americans on the plane and I didn't feel that secure seeing the security guards standing around the airport with machine guns. My enthusiasm started to wane as I definitely wasn't in the USA anymore.

While waiting in the baggage claim area, a nice man approached me and asked if I was Paul Asmuth. It must have been pretty easy to pick me out in the crowd with my blond hair, tan skin, and tall swimmer's physique. I was very glad to meet him.

As we left the airport with my luggage, there was a long corridor, about 15 feet wide, that all arriving passengers had to exit through. The hallway walls were made of patterned bricks that had empty spaces within each brick, just large enough for a child's arm to extend through. As I looked down the passageway, there were hundreds of outstretched arms waving like sea anemones softly swaying in an ocean current, all with their palms open, hoping for anything that may make their lives a bit better. Having never experienced something like this before I found it shocking and heartbreaking. I was definitely feeling out of sorts now.

The late-night traffic was light, and the streets lit with an eerie orange light as we headed to Garden City, a mostly residential area in central Cairo along the east side of the Nile River. The hotel was older but did have a working elevator, for which I was grateful. I tried to be quiet entering the dark room I was sharing with Claudio Plit, from Argentina, and some other swimmers who were already asleep. After finally getting settled in bed to rest, I heard Claudio say, "Only fourteen days until I'm in my home." It was day one and he was already homesick—not such a good sign.

The race organization's headquarters was on an old ferry boat permanently docked across the street from our hotel, on the Nile River. I had no idea what to expect the Nile to look like but the dark, muddy swirling water I peered into was not it. There was nothing about this water that was inviting and I was glad we were not racing in her. We were in Egypt for two races; the first would be in the Suez Canal and the second in the Alexandria Harbor on the Mediterranean Sea. I was confident in my training and experience after a summer of racing. The races didn't offer much prize money and I needed to win both to pay for my travel expenses.

Soon after arriving in Cairo I was introduced to Osama Ahmed Momtaz, who would be helping me during my swims. Osama was a friendly local swimmer; he was a few years younger than me, with a big smile and spoke perfect English. From the first day we met Osama made sure that I had everything I needed to be calm, race well, and begin enjoying my Egyptian experience. He was exactly what I needed and an answer to prayer.

While walking to the pool it seemed like Osama knew everyone we walked by, greeting them with his warm smile and saying, "Praise be to God" or "Peace be with you" in Arabic. Watching and hearing these greetings was comforting to me even though I didn't know what they were saying until later, when Osama and I spoke about the interchanges.

Everyone I met in Cairo and throughout Egypt was gracious and I felt they were genuinely pleased to meet me. The interchanges were similar in asking, "First time to Cairo?" and "Yes, it is," "Welcome to Cairo, we are glad that you are here," and then "Where are you from?" When I told them, "California," their faces would light up with big smiles and they would say, "I love California" or "I love Hollywood." I always came away feeling welcomed.

After a few days in Cairo we traveled by bus to the busy seaport of Port Said (sy-yeed) on the Mediterranean Sea, in the northeast corner of Egypt where the race would start. Port Said was established during the building of the Suez Canal, which opened in 1869. The canal runs 120 miles from Port Said on the north to the city of Suez in the south. The race was to start in the port and then travel south across the harbor, about 8½ miles down the Suez Canal to Ras-el-Esh, where we would turn around and come back. A total distance of 28 kilometers (17 miles). My first out-and-back swim; easy breezy, what could go wrong?

My experience after the first few days in Egypt had been very good, including a camel ride around the pyramids and the incredible sound and light show at the Sphynx. The pyramids and Sphynx are all lit up at night and the show is "narrated" by the Sphynx. Very special to see. The only challenge so far had been recovering from jet lag and finding food that I felt was safe to eat. I had been informed not to consume fresh fruits and vegetables if they hadn't been peeled. Citrus and bananas were okay, but it was hard not to have fresh salads and vegetables. Thankfully I had brought some freeze-dried meals that helped to carry me over when I was hungry.

The morning of the race was calm and Osama and I were well prepared. I had brought everything that I would need for both races. Our escort boats were the traditional small, wooden fishing boats with two rowing stations and a seat in the stern where Osama could sit. Definitely not built for speed but the day was clear and the currents were not expected to be too strong.

The race started early in the morning, at around 8 a.m., and I was the only USA swimmer in the competition. There were athletes from all over the world, but a majority of the swimmers were young Egyptians I knew little about. During the 1950s and 1960s, the Egyptian Abdellatlef Abouheif became the greatest marathon swimmer of the twentieth century, winning marathon swimming races around the globe and establishing world records that still stand today. When I met him, he was a very big and strong man, with an infectious smile and contagious laugh. He always made everyone around him feel welcomed and comfortable with his stories and jokes.

Abouheif (as he was known) was a national hero, recognized wherever he went and had streets and buildings named after him. His achievements catapulted marathon swimming to a premier sport in Egypt. There were many young swimmers in the race who adored Abouheif and wanted to be just like him someday. They were very enthusiastic about competing against me, and I knew that the start would be especially intense.

I also knew that the race would be over 6 hours and the start not very important. However, with all of the young swimmers anxious to impress and nervous, getting quickly into the lead and behind my boat to draft would be a real advantage. Passing another rowing boat once we were in the Suez Canal would be difficult due to the canal's narrow, 200-meter width (a little over 600 feet), plus the length of the oars, leaving little room for the big ships to pass. With this mind-set, when the starter's pistol sounded I took off faster than I would typically begin a 17-mile race.

For the first two miles we crossed the harbor area where large freighters, tankers, barges, and tugboats were docked or maneuvering around. The water was fairly clear, warm, very salty, smelled like diesel fuel, and we had to maneuver around flotsam and jetsam from the ships. The air was filled with engine fumes and I was looking forward to swimming out of this industrial area into the quieter canal.

Swimming next to the huge ships was intimidating, and I focused on my boat and Osama leading us on a good course. Within 45 minutes we were into the Suez Canal, the water was calm and flat with a slight wind to our backs and light, southerly current. I was in the lead with Claudio Plit and Nasser Shazly close by, and I pushed my pace to over 80 strokes per minute. I felt strong and wanted to open up as much of a lead as possible by the halfway turnaround point.

As we swam southward we encountered a convoy of ships heading north, including enormous oil tankers fully loaded with fuel. The ships were as long as 1,000 feet (over three football fields), over 200 feet wide (the canal was only about 600 feet wide), and drafting water 50 feet or more below the ship. The ships were frightening to swim next to as their massive height and girth loomed over me. Now I knew how a tiny bug about to get smashed felt and hoped there was enough room between the ship and the shore for us to swim. In addition to feeling like a speck in the water, as the ships approached, a 6-foot bow wave raised the water level, and then once the ship passed the water level dropped more than 6 feet. Very startling the first time it happened and I was so glad when the ship moved on—and then came another! About a dozen of them—one after the other.

Thankfully the canal was only wide enough for ships to move in one direction at a time. It was one of the more terrifying experiences I had ever felt while swimming. Of course Osama and our fishermen rowers thought nothing of it all, and all they had to say in Arabic was, "*Yallah, yallah!*" ("Hurry up, hurry up!").

With the light wind and helpful southerly current, the trip to the halfway turnaround buoy was fast and we had opened up a good lead of over

10 minutes. The land was now warming faster than the ocean and the heat rising from the land was sucking in the cooler ocean air. These are perfect conditions for a home on the beach, feeling the sea breeze, and not so nice when you have to swim into a headwind.

As soon as we turned the corner everything changed. Suddenly the boat was not able to keep up with my swimming pace as there was now a headwind pushing against us along with the current. There are no locks in the Suez Canal and the current generally flows south in the summer and north in the winter. Between the wind and current we were going to have a long slosh northward to the finish.

Osama was pushing the fishermen as hard as they could go but the boat was not made for swiftness and they were not used to rowing for speed to wherever they went fishing each day. Suddenly, the rowers had to stop and take a break as they were exhausted. I waved to Osama and started swimming north all alone, using the shore of the canal to guide me. Swimming without the boat was a big setback as drafting at the stern allowed me to swim faster; now I was swimming slower and the challengers were closing the gap.

The race official boats were monitoring my progress and location to keep me safe, but now I was worried about when I would be able to feed and hydrate over the next 4 hours. Within what seemed like minutes I saw Osama on my left, running along the banks of the canal with my drinks, and I stopped to refuel. All would be well, I kept telling myself.

Osama and I kept this up for some time until I saw our boat being towed ahead by a powerboat so he could get back in. The boat was back and I was able to start drafting again and pick up my pace, but the rowers and boat just weren't built for the sustained speed that I needed to swim. We repeated the same exercise of losing the boat and Osama running along the shore while keeping an eye on our pursuers.

In most of my marathon swims this year the music playing in my thoughts both encouraged and helped me to pass the time. Right now the only song I could think of was "Mama Told Me Not to Come" by Three

Dog Night, as the day was turning into more of a nightmare and there was still 3 hours to swim.

Osama was relentless in his encouragement, either jogging along the banks of the Suez or the stern of the boat. The race conditions weren't perfect and it was a good day to keep reminding myself that whatever I was feeling and going through, so was everyone else (at least kind of). I pushed as hard as I could, and then as we approached the harbor the wind and current softened and the boat crew was having a better time with the pace. I had probably slowed down a bit, too, after almost 6 hours of racing.

We were now back in the port, passing the same big ships from the morning with only a couple of miles to go. Osama kept encouraging me and the rowers: "*Yallah, yallah.*" We were all exhausted and the finish could not arrive soon enough. Due to his quick thinking and reassurance, we finished the race first after 6 hours and 13 minutes of racing, and boat juggling and coach sprinting. What a day!

A very warm congratulations from our gracious hosts
Photo courtesy of the Long Distance Swimming Federation of Egypt

There is very little alcohol in Egypt, but our hotel at least had a Stella beer that was just perfect for the celebration. Osama abstained. One race down and one to go. Before sleeping that night Claudio let us all know, "Only eight days until I'm in my home."

The next morning, we headed back to Cairo where we could recover and train in the pool for a couple of days. We had found a restaurant with good food not far from our hotel and we ate there every lunch and dinner. It was my first time to have tahini and hummus dishes along with kabobs of different meats, including goat. This is definitely not Florida or California.

Our bus ride through mile after mile of desert (I had never seen so much sand) to Alexandria was uneventful, and we stayed at a nice older hotel overlooking the harbor. Cairo is such a busy, noisy city, with constant car honking, and the seaport of Alexandria felt much more relaxed and California-like. Claudio and I shared a room with a nice view of the race-course venue, inside the safety of the port seawalls and the Mediterranean Sea beyond—quite beautiful.

That first day in Alexandria a group of us went across the street for lunch and sat outside. We were served a beautiful plate of cold, peeled cucumbers and I was craving fresh vegetables. My tablemates assured me that these were safe to eat because they were "peeled." They tasted delicious and I was grateful to have them. Unfortunately this was a mistake.

After an afternoon swim in the harbor I started feeling intestinal discomfort and the resulting effects. I knew that this can be normal when traveling internationally and I wasn't concerned as the race was still three days away. Sadly, the condition continued through the night, and I was unable to sleep and began running a fever in the morning. I didn't swim this day, rested, and hydrated in my hotel room.

By that night the fever had not abated and at the insistence of Osama the race organizers took me to the hospital to see the doctor. The Alexandria hospital was a frightening place for me, so different from any hospital I had seen in the USA. There were invalids in beds along the corridors, because they had no other place to go or people to care for them. My heart ached for their condition.

When I was seen by the doctor, he explained to me that I had an intestinal infection and gave me antibiotics and other medicines to take; he suggested that I might not be able to swim in the race. The doctor let me know that the cucumbers were the most likely culprit for my condition and to stick with cooked vegetables. He was very professional and knowledgeable, and I appreciated his care, and also the concern shown to me by the race committee.

The following day was the day before the race and I stayed in bed and rested, still too weak for a swim. Osama and I spoke about whether to compete or not and decided to make our decision the next day, on race morning.

As I awoke the following morning my fever was gone, and I was feeling better but weak after two days of a high temperature and very little food. I needed to make more money to pay for my airfare home and decided to try to swim the 15-mile race.

The course consisted of eight 3-kilometer (2 miles) rectangular loops around the harbor with buoys that lined the course. All of the coaches had to stay on a dock at the start/finish area, and we would feed each time we came around the course. I knew that normally two miles would take me about 40 minutes to swim; this wasn't ideal for my hydration cycle. I was used to feeding every 20 minutes, and given my weakened state going this long between refueling could present a problem.

We would swim clockwise, always turning to the right. There would only be official and safety boats on the course and the swimmers would be on their own to navigate between the buoys. Thankfully my swimming stroke is efficient and bilaterally symmetrical, so I swim fairly straight. This was important on this type of course as the distance between the course markers was about 200 meters (600-plus feet) and difficult for swimmers to see from one buoy to the next.

To save all of my energy I didn't warm up and just stretched, rested, hydrated, and talked strategy with Osama. I ate a chocolate PowerBar, which was all I could muster, and focused on hydrating. The race contestants were mostly the same as the week before, with a few new young swimmers from the area.

At the start I didn't feel nervous because I wasn't even sure if I would be able to finish and just focused on staying calm. After the starter's pistol sounded I began swimming at a nice, relaxed pace and found myself immediately in the lead. This seemed odd to me as I definitely wasn't starting as fast as the prior weekend's race, yet everyone was letting me break away from the pack. I believe that they thought I was swimming as fast as the week before and normal for me to pull away from them. This I will never know, but I was grateful they let me get ahead.

After the first 2-mile loop I came in to feed and Osama let me know that I had about a 5-minute lead, which was shocking and pleasing. I felt pretty good so I kept the same pace on the next lap, when Osama said the lead was now 10 minutes. This was going better than I thought, and after three laps and 6 miles down, the lead was 15 minutes. *Wow, maybe I can win this*, I thought.

During the fifth lap I started to tire, and during the feed Osama told me that the lead had shrunk to 12 minutes. I nodded, too tired to talk. After six laps the lead was now 8 minutes with two laps to go, and I was fading fast from being ill. Osama was great and encouraging while knowing I was hurting. "You can do this. *Yallah, yallah!*" he yelled, and I knew that whatever I had left needed to come now with 4 miles to go, a little more than 1 hour to finish. *Will my body hold up to finish?*

For the next hour I pushed as hard as I could. With the 2-mile loop allowing a feed only every 40 minutes, this was a huge disadvantage to me right now as my body had no glycogen stores (blood sugar stored in the muscles and liver that endurance athletes tap into during long-distance events) from being sick. Ideally, I really needed calories every 10 minutes. My body was crashing and there wasn't much I could do about it. *Mama told me not to come...* was blasting in my thoughts again. Had I made a mistake to swim today? By continuing to swim did I risk hurting my body even more? I was exhausted and confused.

For most of the laps I had a big lead and couldn't see any swimmers behind me; now I could see them coming, and worse, they could see me. With one lap to go Osama yelled, "Three minutes, your lead is three minutes, *yallah, yallah!*" Could I hold them off for 3 minutes? I was losing 4 or 5 minutes per lap and it wasn't likely. The scenario reminded me of the Tour de France, when the peloton slowly reels in and passes the break-away riders when it seems their lead is insurmountable—always painful to watch.

My stroke rate had been under 80 strokes per minute for many hours and that had never happened in the other swims this summer. There wasn't much I could do about it. My mind knew what was needed to finish, and my body had given up what it had for almost 6 hours already. I focused on swimming as straight and fast as I could stroke after agonizing stroke; stroke, stroke, breathe, stroke, stroke, breathe, check the course, stroke, stroke, breathe. *Do not look back, only look forward to the finish.*

Life is like this sometimes; do we choose to look back at the tough times and let our big bag of regrets drag us down, or look forward to new possibilities and opportunities for good? I had to choose.

As I turned the final buoy with 200 meters to go, I was able to see the swimmers behind me as I breathed to the right; they were less than 50 meters behind. I felt like I was barely moving and they were drawing me in, because they were.

The finish was so close and so were my pursuers. I put my head down and pressed with all I had for the last meters of the race and touched the finish pad first, completely exhausted and needing help to exit the water. Just seconds later, Claudio Plit finished second. Mere seconds after 5 hours and 51 minutes. Amazing.

While many swims of my first summer had tough water conditions of rough, cold, or currents, this one was mentally and physically the hardest. I was a very grateful boy who had just paid for his trip to Egypt. I believe that God isn't all that interested in what place we finish, but is passionate about how we love Him and give Him the glory for each and every day, and I give Him all the glory for keeping me safe today. Thank you, Lord.

Mark Schultz has a song, "He Will Carry Me," and I felt that I had truly been carried through the fires of competition.

My Egyptian experiences would not have been as rewarding or successful without Osama Momtaz. The race committee and Osama were wonderful hosts throughout my stay. Osama went on to an amazing marathon swimming career, including a double crossing of the English Channel in 1984 in 21 hours and 37 minutes (wow!). In 2007, he was inducted into the International Marathon Swimming Hall of Fame. He also earned a PhD from New Mexico State University, Las Cruces, New Mexico.

COACH MARK SCHUBERT

At the advice of my Auburn University swim coach, Eddie Reese, I took a year off collegiate swimming after freshman year. I was a late bloomer and Coach Reese felt that I needed more time to physically mature and recommended training with Mark Schubert in Mission Viejo, California. Some Auburn teammates had trained with the Mission Viejo Nadadores during the summer and informed me of how tough the distance workouts would be. I had no concept of what "tough" really meant and would be training with the distance swimmers in the "animal lane."

I arrived in Mission Viejo in August of 1976, just after the Montreal Olympics. The Nadadores had placed many athletes on the Olympic swimming team; Shirley Babashoff and Brian Goodell had both won gold medals, and Brian set two world records in the 400-meter and 1,500-meter freestyle—my events. Was I intimidated to be training with this national championship team of Olympians, world-record holders, and national champions? Absolutely petrified. In addition, Mark had made an exception to Coach Reese for me to train with his national team, as I had yet to meet the qualifying time standards to compete in the national championships, and I didn't want to let him down, either.

Southern California was very different from Fort Myers, Florida, and especially Mission Viejo. The Saddleback Valley has beautiful rolling hills, with the Cleveland National Forest mountains rising up along the eastern edge. Looking out over this beautiful natural landscape, everything was brown from the summer heat and no rain; in Florida everything was green from constant summer rains. Mission Viejo is one of the biggest planned communities in the United States and all of the homes, roads, recreational centers, golf courses, and landscape were, in my eyes, "perfect" and also new. In 1976, there were houses being built everywhere with future homeowners waiting in lines to snap them up. Demand was causing home prices to rise so fast buyers were sometimes selling their new home to another buyer while still in escrow, eager to make a quick profit, a strategy called "flipping." What a different world from which I had come. And there was only one country music station on the radio.

Mark is a man of few words on the pool deck—all business. All of my coaches up to this time had easygoing personalities both on and off the pool deck, and I felt a close friendship with them. This was not Mark; he was very serious. From the first day of the new training year he barked out directions as soon as practice started. Gone was the friendly banter I was used to, and Mark was perfectly clear that we were there to work and not socialize. Once practice started, there was no talking. *Wow, no talking? What had I gotten myself into?* I had made many tough decisions to move from Florida to California, and my parents were also sacrificing financially to support me. *Had I made a big mistake?*

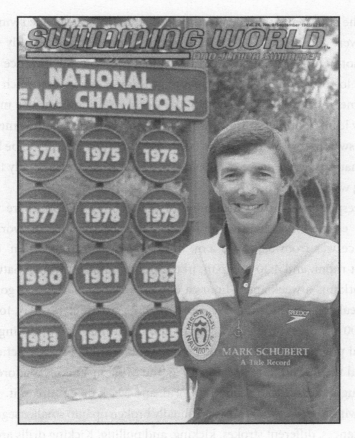

Mark Schubert
Photo Courtesy of *Swimming World* magazine

Once we started a swimming set Mark would pace around the four corners of the pool like a mountain lion about to pounce. If we swam 6 miles in the workout, he must have walked 12 miles. We never knew where he was because he was constantly moving and noticed everything going on in the pool. If we were lazy on a turn at the wall or used our arms to propel us forward during a kicking-only drill, he noticed and would let us KNOW! Serious offenders would be sent home from practice. I had come a long way from wanting to get kicked out of practice. I did my best to follow Mark's instructions at every workout and compete with the other swimmers in the animal lane.

The summer Nadadores team included many college-age swimmers who were all now back at their universities, and so I was the only swimmer not in high school. This didn't feel that great but the distance group had a lot of very speedy high school swimmers who were much faster than me, including Brian Goodell, the world record holder, and my new reality leading our lane. This group of tough young men and women distance swimmers would push me every day over the next year to be better, and that was why I drove over 3,000 miles to be here. I was really feeling a long way from home.

Despite it being the beginning of the training season, there wasn't much easing into the swimming distances or number of workouts. Practice was from 5:30 to 8 a.m. in the pool, 3:30 to 4:30 p.m. in the weight room, and 4:30 to 7 p.m. in the pool, Monday through Saturday; 12 workouts a week and 5 hours a day of swimming. This was going to be a real challenge for me. We swam 20,000 yards/meters a day, totaling 120,000 per week, the equivalent of about 75 miles of swimming. Any missed practice had to be made up on Sunday. I didn't miss practice as I needed the day off to recover. In 1976, the Mission Viejo Nadadores was the toughest place to train in the world, and Mark made sure of it.

Swimming workouts are traditionally broken up into smaller segments of distances, different strokes, kicking, and pulling. Kicking drills are usually done with both arms holding onto a small floating board so only your legs are free to propel. Pulling drills involve binding our feet together with a rubber strap or small tube, plastic paddles strapped to our hands, and a small flotation buoy between the thighs to keep our hips afloat.

Within these segments and drills, the distances are often broken up into multiple lengths of the pool, leaving on a specific time interval. For instance, to swim 1,000 yards a coach may ask the swimmers to swim 10 times 100 yards (100 yards is 4 lengths of a 25-yard pool). After each 100 yards there would be a short rest. The coach may say the set is 10 × 100s, leaving on an interval of every 1 minute and 10 seconds. If it takes 1 minute to swim 100 yards, the swimmer would have 10 seconds to rest before pushing off and doing another 100 yards until all 10 were completed.

Sample from my daily log book of a tough training day
with the Mission Viejo Nadadores

One morning Mark came over to the animal lane and told us to swim 4,000 yards by swimming a set of 10 × 400 yards, leaving every 4 minutes and 20 seconds. A very hard set for our group at that time and we all thought that this would be the hardest and main set of the workout. We got through this tough set and were spent. Then to teach us mental toughness, Mark told us that we were going to swim another set of 10 × 400 yards leaving every 4 minutes and 10 seconds. We were all in shock! And then, by digging deep into our physical and mental reserves, we made it. He was very good at expecting more from us than we thought we could deliver, and we would do it because he believed that we could, and we believed in him. Exactly what a great coach should do.

One Saturday when all of the swimmers were tapering for a high school swim meet I trained with Ed Ryder, a high school senior who had also come from Florida. Ed was a fellow distance swimmer and not entered in the meet, so I had one training partner that day, and lots of Mark's attention. Ed and I swam 11,000 yards in the morning, and then came back that night for what we hoped would be a shorter workout as it was just Mark, Ed, and me.

A short workout was not in the cards that afternoon, and after swimming 11,000 more yards that Saturday we were exhausted and expecting Mark to tell us to loosen down and go home. Instead, Mark asked us to swim an extremely hard set of 10 × 75 yards, leaving every 45 seconds. Wow! And then he said, "You aren't going home until you make all ten." Unbelievable! I was being asked to swim one of the fastest sets of my career, at the end of one of the hardest training days of my life, at the end of another huge week of yardage, and I didn't believe I could make it.

Ed was a faster swimmer than me and made 8 or 9 of the 75s on our first attempt and I made 4 or 5, not believing that I could make all 10. To my surprise Mark was true to his word: we weren't going home. He made us start the 10 × 75s over again. This time I made 6 and Ed almost made all again at 8 or 9. We were toast!

The Eagles had just released their Hotel California album, and by this point I felt trapped like the lyrics from the song "Hotel California" when they sing you can check out anytime you like, but you can never leave.

Mark got in our faces as only he could do, with the stare of a cobra about to strike, and said, "You can make this; ten, seventy-fives, on forty-five seconds. NOW LET'S GO!" Would we be "checking out"? It looked like we certainly weren't leaving.

Somewhere deep inside of me I found the courage and strength needed to complete all 10 of the 75s on 45 seconds on my third try, and Ed did, too. Neither of us had believed we could make the set, but Mark knew that we could if we believed that we could. Again he showed us that he believed we could accomplish the set and we believed in him. We both swam more than 23,000 yards that day, about 20 miles, with the hardest set being the last.

Days of training like this with Mark over the years would prepare me for a sport of which I had no knowledge or aspirations. My focus each day was to simply to do my very best and enjoy each workout with my teammates.

During the fall of my first year in Mission Viejo, a coach named Don Swartz from Marin, California, came to speak to the entire team about mental preparation. Don was a swim coach as well as a trainer for the Creative Performance Institute that he founded, to teach the mental side of sports. The seminars were the most mind-opening experiences of my life thus far.

Where Coach Gregg Troy had taught us to think outside the box for success and had us read books like *Jonathan Livingston Seagull* by Richard Bach, Don was teaching us how the brain worked to influence positive outcomes. And most importantly, how to get our brains working for us to achieve our greatest potential in the pool and in life.

I learned that when I closed my eyes and imagined my success in a swimming race while incorporating this imagery along with the senses I would feel at that moment, I was training my brain to help me succeed; this is because our conscious and subconscious brain functions don't distinguish the difference between real versus imagined achievements. Attaching my emotions and senses is key so that the same areas of the brain are being activated as if the actual event were happening. Just like back in Fort Myers when I practiced feeling the emotions of the first time I would beat my then nemesis, Jeff Evans.

Similar to the work that Don Swartz was doing, Lou and Diane Tice founded the Pacific Institute in Seattle in 1971. Lou and the Pacific Institute has worked with many sports and business teams in over sixty countries around the globe. Here is a quote from Lou:

Visualization and Your Goals

"How important is mental preparation when it comes to achieving a goal that is within your reach?

"When you decide on a goal that you want to achieve, when you know it is possible and you feel strongly committed to getting it done, what is next? What can you do that will help ensure positive results?

"Well, the first thing you need to do is remind yourself not to get bogged down in figuring out 'how' you are going to achieve it. The 'how' is important, but it doesn't come first. First, you want to clearly and vividly visualize the end result. The more clearly and more often you see it (and when I say 'see it,' I mean feel it, taste it, smell it and make it 100% real in your imagination), the more likely it is to become real in the world.

"It takes energy to create reality from a vision or idea, but it happens all the time. Every single person-made reality in the world first started out as an idea inside someone's head. The more thought, the more energy – and the more energy, the more likely the reality.

"Professional athletes know this and use visualization techniques all the time. I've been teaching it for more than 27 years. Now, there is research accumulation to back it up. Nowadays these techniques are used in medicine, psychology, and education and by more and more folks just like you and me.

"Where the thought goes, energy flows. If you can clearly see it, you are far more likely to really be it. Keep that in mind as you move toward your goals."

After college graduation, the 1980 Olympic boycott, and becoming a professional athlete, I continued to train with the Nadadores through 1985, when Mark left for Mission Bay, Florida. Over these years my relationship with Mark grew into a valued friendship, especially years after college when I was training with swimmers a decade younger than me.

Each summer swim season there would be a great group of talented young distance swimmers in our Mission Viejo animal lane who were excellent athletes. Regularly one of these young bucks would want to come and train in the open water with me, thinking that it must be easier than the pool workouts Mark was demanding of them. Mark and I always encouraged anyone to come to the lake or ocean to accompany me for a 2-hour or more open water workout. I enjoyed being pushed in training by these great young athletes and it was a nice break for them, as well. The revelation for the pool swimmer was how hard the open water workouts were and how they suffered in their next pool workout, sometimes unable to complete the afternoon training. They were unusually tired and sore from having to hold their bodies in one position for so long with no breaks for turns, lifting their heads for direction, and swimming non-stop for a long period of time. Their necks, lower backs, and core muscles would all be aching from this new type of swimming experience. Mark and I would later laugh as no one ever asked to train open water with me more than once.

Training in Lake Mission Viejo
Photo courtesy of *Swimming World* magazine

Once Mark and I understood the amount and type of training needed to truly excel in open water swimming, we created specific workout goals. On some days, when Mark, his wife Joke (pronounced Yoka), and daughters Tatum and Leigh would go waterskiing in Lake Elsinore, I would go for open water workouts. I would train 2 hours in the morning, swim 2 hours in the lake while the Schubert family was water skiing, and then workout another 2 hours at afternoon pool practice. These were long and hard training days, exactly what I needed to get ready for this extreme marathon sport I had chosen.

Mark and I stayed in touch, and when he was the University of Texas women's head coach, he invited me to join his team for altitude training at the US Olympic Training Center in Colorado Springs, Colorado, in 1990 and 1991. Years later, Mark was the USA Swimming national team director, and he asked me to join USA Swimming as an advisor for the open water national team. During this time I had the honor of coaching and advising great USA open water athletes from 2007 to 2012, including the 2008 Beijing and 2012 London Olympics.

I will forever be grateful for the thousands of miles Mark coached me from the pool deck, at swim meets, and our continued friendship. But most of all I will treasure him for how he believed in me before I was ready to believe in myself.

La Traversee du Lac Memphremagog

1982

"Oh, Paul. Oh, Paul."

The beautiful, glacially formed lake running 26 miles from Newport, Vermont, to Magog, Quebec, is Lac Memphremagog. Three-fourths of the lake's watershed are in Vermont and flow from the Clyde, Barton, Black, and Johns Rivers. The lake waters flow slowly northward, emptying into the Magog River, which joins the Saint Francois River, eventually empties into the Saint Lawrence River and ultimately in the Atlantic Ocean. Lac Memphremagog meant "where there is a big expanse of water" in the native Abenaki tribe and Algonkian language.

The fresh water lake is about 350 feet at the deepest and local folklore claims there is a serpent-like monster named "Memphre" that lives in these waters. If true, Memphre may be a member of the extinct aquatic reptile Sauropterygia or a plesiosaurs, another extinct marine reptile and most likely what Nessie the creature of Loch Ness is. So they could be distantly related, along with Champy the Lake Champlain lake monster that lives only 70 miles to the west.

For Memphre, there were as many as eight documented sightings dating back to the early 1800s and are part of the First Nations legends. In 1997, the nearby University of Sherbrooke released data by Sonia Bolduc stating there had been 215 well-documented sightings of Memphre.

The novel *The Sea Serpent Legend* by Norman Bingham, published in 1926, describes the lake monster and offers a poem as follows:

> "They saw a monster dark and grim,
> Coming with coiling surge and swim,
> With lifted head and tusk and horn,
> Fierce as the spirit of Hades born."

The cold water, distance, and fear of Memphre may have been some of the reasons that kept anyone from swimming Lac Memphremagog for centuries, and a lake monster surely kept the First Nation fisherman out of her waters. Almost two years before I was born, on August 21, 1955, William Francis "Billy" Connor (a twenty-year-old Canadian sailor home on leave in Magog) lowered himself into the water in Newport, Vermont, at 4:30 in the afternoon to try to become the first person to ever swim the 26-mile-long lake.

Billy swam valiantly through the night, including a thunderstorm that caused his escort craft to lose sight of him for a time. The storm darkened the lake and sky, yet Billy's spirits were raised when the homes along the eastern shore guided his way by all turning on their outside lights for him. The town was so enthralled that the Roman Catholic Mass was dismissed early so the congregation and most of the town could be there to meet him. It was a real team and town effort by everyone to help Billy finish this amazing feat. After 18 hours and 35 minutes in the water, this hometown hero was able to walk out of the water unaided to the cheers of thousands and became the first person to ever conquer the lake.

It was in 1979 when the Magog Labatt beer distributor, George Lussier, organized the first professional marathon swim from Prouty Beach, Newport, to Parc de la Pointe-Merry beach in Magog, a distance of 42 kilometers (26 miles). George was a small bundle of everlasting energy and constant movement, with good English and a flowing fountain of positivity. His proposed race distance would be the longest marathon swimming race in the world without current aid (the annual Argentina swim down the Rio Coronda is longer at 57 kilometers, with swimmers aided by swift currents along the way).

The World Professional Marathon Swimming Federation (WPMSF) wasn't sure how long it would take the athletes to complete the distance and there was less total prize money offered to the swimmers for such a long race. With this in mind, an agreement was made between the race organizers and WPMSF that the race would "officially" end at a point approximately 37 kilometers (23 miles) from the start and the finish places determined at that point. If swimmers wanted to swim the final 5 kilometers (3 miles) to the beach, that was their choice.

John Kinsella "won" the 1979 event by being the first to the official finish point and promptly jumped into his boat and exited the lake. Claudio Plit, swimming second, and many of the other marathon swimmers decided to complete the crossing of the lake and finished at the Magog Parc de la Pointe-Merry beach to the adoration of thousands of fans. The race organizers were thrilled and the first-year event was a success. A lot of Labatt beer was sold and George was very happy!

The following summer of 1980, James Kegley and I had competed in every race available to us in our inaugural season, and we were tired. Here is a summary of what we had done so far:

- July 6: 23 miles – Around the Island Swim, Atlantic City (first and second place)
- July 19–20: 70 miles – 24 Hours of La Tuque (we each swam 35 miles, first place)
- July 23: 6 miles – Lac St. Jean qualification (first and second place)
- July 27: 21 miles – *La Traversee du Lac St. Jean* (first and second place)
- August 3: 6 miles – *Les Quatorze Milles de Paspebiac* (both did not finish)

We had been trying to get confirmation from the race organizer, George Lussier, about entering the race after the Lac St. Jean event and he was not allowing it. Thankfully with media pressure from Richard Chartier at *La Presse*, Moe Jacobs from the *Newport Daily News* and Bertrand Gosselin, a Sherbrooke and Magog radio announcer (who became a lifelong friend), the race organizers allowed for a 10-kilometer qualification for two additional swimmers to qualify. On August 6 (my birthday), James and I finished first and second in the qualifier, and entered the 1980 Lac Memphremagog race. Congratulations! We got to swim with a lake monster! Not sure we should have been so excited.

We went on to finish first and third in the race, and I established the first "official" crossing record of 9 hours and 51 minutes, 47 minutes faster than Claudio's unofficial race record from the previous summer. The lake had her way of completely tiring out many of the swimmers and only ten of the twenty-one swimmers who started in the morning at Prouty Beach finished this day.

Finish of the 1980 race with a very joyful George Lussier
Photo courtesy of *La Traversee Internationale du Lac Memphremagog*

For James and me, it was an exhausting and successful summer for our introductory season of marathon swimming. Including the Lac Memphremagog crossing, we had each raced over 120 miles in the five weeks between July 6 and August 10. That was a lot of open water swimming.

Thinking back to the first race of the summer in Atlantic City, I had learned so much and felt so blessed to have the opportunity to represent my country. It wasn't the Olympic dream I had been chasing, but in some ways it was better for me. If I had made the Olympic team, I most likely would not have won a medal. In Atlantic City and Quebec, I had thousands of people cheering for me at the finish and our pictures were on the front page of the Quebec newspapers. Along with the other marathon swimming titans, I was a champion for completing these unbelievably hard events, something so few in the world would ever be able to do. We were heroes. I was very satisfied and happy with the summer.

The Quebec races were like competing in a Super Bowl every weekend. Media events, meet-and-greet events, parades, and lots of free stuff. Most of the races that summer were sponsored by one of the larger breweries of the time, Molson, Labatt, and Laurentides. At every race event there was food and beer offered complimentary to the athletes, and for two young men just out of college, James and I were in heaven; it reminded me of Coach Gregg Troy teaching me SMBWIF (so much better when it's free)! There were no expectations on us that first summer; we had the time of our lives and won enough prize money to pay all of our travel expenses and take home a little bit, too. A good (and tough) summer job.

The modern town of Magog was established in 1776 when a group of loyalist emigrated from Vermont. With an English-speaking background and a race start in the USA, it was the event location where I felt most at home. The race organizers and volunteers were always so kind and generous to the athletes, making sure that we were well provisioned. Media events and parades along with meet-and-greet opportunities were well attended and local fans had easy access to the swimmers, leading to long-term friendships.

A friend, fan, and writer for the local newspaper *Le Soleil d'Orford*, Lynn Blouin published an article about what it means to be a volunteer for this race and I asked her to interpret:

I Don't Swim
By Lynn Blouin
General Secretary for International Marathon Swimming Association
Race Director for La Traversee du Lac Memphremagog
and...friend"

I don't, really!

I mean, of course I can go around a pool for a couple of laps or jump in and out of the ocean when on vacation but...I wouldn't call it swimming. Not after you've seen what those guys do.

I was only a teenager in my hometown of Magog, Quebec, Canada, when a small group of promotors came up with this idea for a new summer event; they would have a bunch of swimmers coming from all around the world to swim the 42 km distance of Lake Memphremagog (Indian name that means "great body of water") from Newport, Vermont, USA to Magog, Quebec, Canada.

Right!

So as hundreds of others, I stood there for hours just waiting to see if ONE of them would make it alive. And the miracle happened; as it has now for 20 years this summer.

First as a local fan and then as a young journalist, I stood there, year after year, wondering... So I decided to get a little closer and join the volunteer group, hundreds of them, that make it all possible, and that's when IT really HAPPENED. Let me explain...

Every year, the volunteers that have already been around make it a tradition to take the new ones close enough so they can witness, firsthand, the finish of the race. Now, you especially want to take the ones that have put the extra effort or the others that have threatened to quit a couple of times when things got a little too demanding. The trick is to have them stand there while one of the swimmer's is coming in. You have them as close as possible and you just watch for the signs...

Although they can be cheering, they usually are speechless. They won't move or blink an eye as the swimmer touches the finish line, comes out of the water and disappears into the medical facilities. Then they turn to you (watery eyes are common here) and tell you with that low tone of voice that gives away the lump they have in their throat, "OK, now I get the reason why we're doing all of this." It was now twelve years ago and I've gone since from Public Relations committees to Vice President, President, Delegate to International Affairs, to my latest responsibility, Race Director.

This thing is, once one has witnessed the extraordinary demonstration of how far the human body can be pushed, hour after hour, in weather conditions that can go from tropical paradise to natural catastrophe in a minute; once one has learned that, in order to achieve that, those athletes have to train daily for hours, most of the time alone, and subtract themselves from many of life's simplest pleasures; once one has realized the psychological and emotional strength and courage those people have to build to face such an ordeal, then you can't help but have the deepest respect for each of them and want to do something, anything, to help them achieve their goal.

And when they set foot in the water on the morning of a race or roll their arms around like an old airplane for a last stretch before they go or lay their head back and close their eyes after touching the finish line... It's a little like being there yourself... Except you don't swim!

When I turned thirty years old in 1987, the town held a birthday party in my honor under the big-event tent. I was humbled by the turnout and the 30-foot-long cake. The people of Magog always made the swimmers feel very special.

The crossing of Lac Memphremagog was a race where I enjoyed some of my best racing success. The lake waters were typically between 68 and 72 degrees and the weather warmer than the other Quebec races, with pristine water and good visibility to 15 feet. The long, narrow lake prevented large waves from forming even when battling against headwinds, although when these northerly winds occurred they easily added an hour to the finish time and gave me the feeling of softly beating my head against the wall all day. *Thump, thump, thump!* It felt so good when it stopped.

These attributes of temperature, water quality, and less wave action were very beneficial to converted and fast pool swimmers like James Kegley and me, and then later Bill and Rob Schmidt, former University of California at Berkeley swimmers, and Tom Wiley, a former Arizona State University swimmer. With calmer and temperate water, I would focus exclusively on swimming fast and not so much on dealing with the elements. My race strategies were typically to start the swim at a strong pace of 80-plus strokes per minute and try to build faster as I went through the day.

By moving to the front early in the race and trying to extend a lead of ½ mile or more (about a 10-minute lead), I would be able to control the race pace while keeping a careful watch for anyone making a move to catch me. My goal was to get the other competitors to give up quickly on winning and start thinking about second place.

Once in a comfortable lead and with so much time to think, songs would regularly fill my mind, especially "Midnight Rider" by the Allman Brothers Band; I would change the key lyrics from "midnight rider" to "marathon swimmer": "*You ain't gonna catch the marathon swimmer*"— and they usually never did. In 1983, Donna Summer released "She Works Hard for the Money," and while the lyrics didn't mean much to me the refrain definitely did, as I was working VERY hard for the money!

At times when I wanted to really push hard in a race, I would imagine a strong cable attached to my head that led all the way to the finish line, or at back of the boat when drafting behind a rowing boat. This cable would virtually pull me forward, easing the pain in my arms and speeding me along toward the finish.

Keeping focused was key during such a long race because the unchanging, beautiful, and boreal forest that surrounds the lake and covers the mountains was at times monotonous. Despite the intensity of competition, maintaining concentration mile after excruciating mile is challenging after so many hours. The shoulders and lower back pain was a constant companion after a few hours and helped to keep me alert. At least there were no sharks or jellyfish to concern me.

There is a large mountain along the western lakeshore just inside the Canadian border, Mont Owl's Head, that you can see from everywhere in the region, including the race start and finish. This ski resort mountain has an altitude of 2,451 feet, rising almost 2,000 feet above the lake level. While swimming toward the mountain, I feel like I will never arrive. While swimming alongside Mont Owl's Head, I feel like it will take forever to move past her. And once beyond the mountain, if I looked back she would make me feel like I wasn't moving at all. I learned not to look at the mountain.

About 10 miles north of Mont Owl's Head is the picturesque Saint Benedictine monastery, Saint-Benoit-du-Lac. The abbey is home to about fifty monks who make cheese for sale to local restaurants and merchants. The church spires were always a welcome sight for me, knowing that I was more than halfway to the finish, and I would push even harder from this point on. Knowing how the monks devoted their entire lives to taking care of God's creation was inspiring to me.

Most of my years racing in Magog, I stayed with the family of Pierre Paul and Andree Landreville. Together they ran a local restaurant, Les Trois Marmites (the Three Pots). The food was excellent, fresh, and plentiful, so the swimmers would often go there for meals if not required to be elsewhere for media appearances. Pierre Paul, Andree, and their daughters Martine, Annick, and Genevieve, and son Phillipe were excellent hosts and fans of all of the swimmers; they became my Magog family. I always felt having a "family" that I looked forward to seeing each summer, and who shared their love with me each racing season, gave me such an advantage over the other athletes. I was competing for my "hometown" crowd. What more could I ever hope for than a loving, caring, and relaxing home to prepare for an excruciatingly long day of racing?

Pierre Paul bought fresh cheese for Les Trois Marmites from the Benedictine monks and had become friends with the monastery's abbot. They developed a close relationship over the years; Pierre Paul would speak to the abbot about the race and the swimmers each summer, and I knew that the monks were praying and singing Gregorian chants for all of our safety as we swam by their beautiful estate. Knowing that their prayers were with us mattered a lot to me and I would pick up the pace from here to the finish. This is one reason why we selected the photo of me swimming by the monastery for the book's cover.

In 1982, my dad decided that he wanted to come up to Quebec and see what the marathon swimming racing was all about. My mom had been to her first race that summer in Atlantic City and Dad wanted to have his turn, too. There couldn't have been a better town for Dad to meet and mingle with the locals. Being the pastor of large churches during his career, one of the things that he did best was meeting people. By the end of the week in Magog he knew more people than I did, and remembered all of their names, too, a wonderful gift he possessed. For years after being in Magog, he would ask, "How's Bert? How's Jacques?" Magog was his town now, too.

The logistics of the race that year are not memorable to me, but the finish is. At the finish of the Quebec marathons, there would always be thousands of people cheering for us and Magog had a big beach area where 20,000 people could watch us arrive. The race course was designed so that we had to swim a 1,000-meter "sprint" (pretty hard to really go fast after 9 hours of swimming, but we did our best) in the finish area and there was extra prize money for the fastest time. (James Kegley usually won these.)

There would be a series of buoys and markers so that we would follow a path, allowing most everyone on the beach to see us swim closely past. As a swimmer this was such an exciting feeling, to hear the roar of 15,000 or more people (fueled by a long day of drinking beer) cheering for us to swim as fast as we could the final stage of the race. Near the end of the sprint area there was a 90-degree turn and then the final 50-meter distance to where we would touch the finish pad. This pad was typically a large, 4-feet high by 6-feet wide clear plastic board supported vertically above the water by floatation devices attached to a long floating dock full of media, race organizers, politicians, medics, and volunteers. Someone over the years had the idea of making the pad clear for improved photography, a good concept for everyone to see the finish better.

Finish of *La Traversee Internationale du Lac Memphremagog*

Like my previous two years in Magog, 1982 had huge throngs and the energy from the crowds always palpable. To raise your arms in victory after 9 hours of pushing yourself to the limit and hearing their voices all raising up for you, is the most incredible athletic moment I would ever experience. It felt like I could just float out of the water, lifted by the love of everyone watching. My body covered in goose bumps, a smile extending from ear to ear, and tears rolling down my face. I bet heaven feels like this every day.

I often think while watching important World Series baseball games, where the batter clinches the game with a walk off home run, that this is how I feel at the end of winning big races, except I had just swam 9 hours and was completely exhausted.

On this day in 1982, the finish was even more special; there on the end of the dock was my dad, taking it all in—a very proud day for him and an experience I was so glad he could feel. I will always remember that when I exited the water, the first person to hug me was my dad and he was sobbing uncontrollably, and all he could say between sobs was, "Oh, Paul. Oh, Paul." He was fifty-three that summer and I'm sure it was a memory he never forgot. I know I never will. I had only seen my dad cry twice in my life, during unhappy situations, and it was an amazing feeling to share these happy tears together.

Dad and I were able to share the same special moment again in 1983, with my sister Cindi coaching me from the boat all day. A very joyous family affair.

Sweet hugs from my dad at the finish of the 1982 race
Photo courtesy of *Le Progres*, Magog, Quebec

The twentieth anniversary of the race was held in 1998. After not competing since 1992, I devoted my summer to racing one more time in Magog. It was a first for Team Asmuth.

Team Asmuth at the 1998 finish: Logan, Kendall, Paul, and Marilyn; on my right is Jocelyn Proulx, and left of Marilyn is Martin Dussault, president of *La Traversee*, and Fetalo!
Photo courtesy of *La Traversee Internationale du Lac Memphremagog*

Thank you, Dad, Team Asmuth, and thank you to everyone who ever made Magog, Newport, and participating in *La Traversee Internationale du Lac Memphremagog* such an amazing experience to race, to visit, and of which to be part. You shared your soul and community with me for just a short time each year for over twelve summers. You made all of us feel loved, and we will be forever grateful.

COACH RON "THE ROCK"
JOHNSON

"Our sport is a performance art. When done well, it is infused with emotion, willingness to break personal barriers, and inspiration to go where no one has gone before."

This quote by Coach Ron Johnson is from his book *Romancing the Water* and gives us just a small glimpse into how his mind worked. Ron was the Arizona State University head swim coach during my years beginning in August 1977 to graduation in May 1980. They were some of the most wonderful and tumultuous years of my life.

Ron was known as "the Rock" because he was a tall, muscular man who kept in supreme physical and mental condition, and was a phenomenal athlete his whole life. He was quick to smile, laugh, and make a joke of his quirkiness, putting everyone else around him at ease. Some of Ron's eccentricities arose from his brilliant and creative mind. I had never been around a coach who was as fun, smart, imaginative, inspirational, and disciplined. Swim practices were a joy to look forward to, even knowing they were going to be extremely challenging.

On the first day of practice Ron already had prepared a notebook with every workout for the entire season completed. He would spend his summer in preparation for the year ahead. Each training group would be different—sprinters, middle distance, backstroke, butterfly, and breast-stroke specialist, and my group, the distance swimmers. If I wanted to see how tough the Christmas break workouts were going to be, I could flip forward to late December or early January and there the grueling sessions would be waiting. I never looked forward; today's tough workout was enough to be concerned about. In all of my years of swimming, I've never known a coach with as much brilliance as Ron.

Each afternoon workout would start the same on the swimming pool deck. A group of forty young men and women, with tanned skin from training in the Arizona sun and strong muscles from the miles of laps and hours of lifting weights, would loosen up, stretching their muscles to Ron's routine. "Swing right arm forward" and we would all windmill our arms in big circles like a plane propeller. "Left arm forward, left arm back..." We were an eclectic group, just like our coach, and acted like a big loving family that supported and watched out for each other.

Not all personality types worked well with Ron's style of personal accountability and creativity. If you came to college to party and missed practice, your time line was going to be short on the ASU swim team. As the saying in coaching circles goes, "You can't hoot with the owls if you want to soar with the eagles." In other words, you better get to bed early if you want to be up and ready for 6 a.m. morning practices.

After my year with Mark Schubert in Mission Viejo, where we swam more than 60 miles a week, I knew that training at ASU was not going to be as hard. However, what I encountered was a coach who required more of me by helping to open up my mental capabilities for success. This was hard work, too, and required discipline to achieve.

Ron was an early pioneer of meditation and visualization. We would lay on the locker room floor before practice and listen to meditations Ron had prerecorded for us. We would hear his soothing voice tell us to "slow down your breathing," "allow the healing blue light to enter your body," "experience the emotions and feelings as you touch the wall, winning the race." These meditations helped train our minds for success and were just as important as our physical preparations.

Ron was also on the cutting edge of medicinal health ideas, or at least he thought so, and we were a good group to test on. Whenever we were sick he had us drink a noxious-smelling tea from the creosote bush that grew in the Arizona desert near campus. The tea tasted like the smell of a wooden telephone pole dipped in tar, and left a light-green tinge on our teeth and tongues. He also had us eat raw garlic for the natural antibiotic capabilities in the clove. Wow, did we smell bad sometimes with the odor of garlic oozing out of our pores. If we couldn't outswim our competitors, we could knock them back a bit with our breath. At least we had that going for us.

Prior to becoming the ASU head coach, Ron had lived in Mexico City and was the Mexican national team's head coach from 1966 to 1973, including the 1968 and 1972 Olympics. During this time, he coached Guillermo Echevarria to a world record in the 1,500-meter freestyle. This was my best event and the most probable way to qualify for the USA Olympic team in 1980. Ron knew how to coach distance swimmers; all of our focus during my years at ASU was geared toward my Olympic dream.

Under Ron's guidance, and the tremendous training background I had from Coaches Troy and Schubert, I rapidly progressed at ASU from not scoring any points at a national championship to becoming a three-time NCAA All-American, finishing fourth place at the NCAA championships in my last two years of college. With the top three finishers qualifying for an Olympic berth at the upcoming trials, I knew that with a great swim I could make the team. Ron felt so, too.

1980 NCAA Swimming Championships with Ron,
Harvard University, Cambridge, Massachusetts
Photo courtesy of ASU teammate Sam Jones

Growing up in Fort Myers, Florida, I was always outdoors—swimming, camping, hiking, hunting, fishing, waterskiing, at the beach, and many other outdoor activities that the southwest coast of Florida invites. Indoor activities were primarily limited to Miami Dolphin football games on Sunday afternoon TV. When it came time to decide what my career path was going to be in college I chose wildlife management, both for my love of the natural sciences as well as believing that a majority of the job would be focused outdoors. There was one career I definitely knew I didn't want to ever have, and that was accounting.

In Fort Myers, the Highway 41 bridge that crosses the Caloosahatchee River is about 70 feet above the water to allow large boats to pass beneath.

This is the same highway that the Allman Brothers Band sings about in "Ramblin' Man," being born in the backseat of a Greyhound bus that is rolling down Highway 41. One of my best friends in high school was Cliff Betts; his cousin Dickey Betts was part of the Allman Brothers Band. We loved that Southern rock music.

Before I could drive, I rode my bike everywhere, on most days more than 20 miles. Riding gave me the independence that I longed for at a young age. The Highway 41 bridge was for cars only; pedestrians and bicyclists were prohibited. Seeing myself as a real speed demon on my Schwinn 10-speed bike, and with no hills around in the flatness of the Florida Gulf Coast, I may have decided to cross the bridge a time or two. Not saying for sure, but the bike speeds achieved on the downhill slopes were exhilarating, practically keeping up with the cars.

The bridge is right next to the city's "financial district" (not much at the time), and when you reach the bridge's apex it is easy to see into the downtown buildings. At this time there was only one tall office structure. In the predawn hours on our way to early morning swim practice or on our way home after nightfall, there was usually only one office whose lights regularly pierced the darkness. I would ask my mom or dad when we drove by, "Whose office is that with the lights on all the time?"

And they would say, "That's our friend Charlie Taylor. He's a CPA."

"What's that?" I asked.

"A certified public accountant. He takes care of people's finances and taxes."

That's all I needed to hear. From then on I knew if there was one profession I would never want to pursue it was to become an accountant. Be indoors hours and hours every day? That was not for me.

ASU had a great wildlife management major and was a key reason that attracted me to the university. I loved the major and everything that I was learning, and then reality hit. Three semesters before graduation I had to take 15 hours of classroom time each week and 15 hours of laboratory time each week. Class time was no issue, the big problem was all of the lab hours were during afternoon swim practice and missing training time wouldn't work for Olympic preparation. Plus, I needed my swimming scholarship to stay in school. Now what? Almost done with school and I needed to find a new career? Wow. I was bummed out.

My other career interest had been in law enforcement, to become either a game warden or possibly join the FBI. For many years my dad had been chaplain for the Fort Myers Police Department and wrote about these experiences in his book, *Preacher with a Billy Club*. In this capacity he had gotten to know the two Lee County FBI Agents well. Dad set up a lunch for the four of us and the two agents did a great job of encouraging me to pursue a career path for the bureau. In addition, they let me know most crimes were now accomplished by "white collar" types of criminals, and the best pathway for me would either be a law or accounting degree. Accounting? Wow, this was the last thing I wanted to do, but going to law school would be worse. I knew I was good at math; I switched majors to accounting. Unbelievable.

ASU has the renowned W. P. Carey School of Business, which has an excellent accounting program. I had only three semesters until graduation and now had to work extra hard to "catch up" in a new major. Summer school would be required, too. Just when I was looking forward to a light class load gearing up to the 1980 Olympic trials.

While no longer learning about my passions for the environment and studying ecosystems, the accounting major went well while learning about debits and credits, balance sheets, and cash flow statements. At least I was on track to graduate in May of my last year and the FBI was an exciting career option.

As part of my extracurricular activities, I had joined a campus accounting association that met monthly. There were industry speakers who would come and talk with our group, mostly about the career path of becoming a CPA (something I knew wasn't for me, I was going into the FBI). In my last semester, a young FBI agent was invited to speak with our accounting group and for the first time I was very excited to hear what one of our speakers had to say. He was clean cut with a very smart suit, just like the FBI agents on the TV show. All was well. Then he started talking about his career over the last seven years and that he had lived in five major cities during this time—Dallas, Washington D.C., Miami, Los Angeles, and now Phoenix. WHAT? Alarm bells were going off in my head.

The two agents I met in Fort Myers had been there for many years and never mentioned having to relocate several times during their careers. One thing that I knew about myself is that moving from city to city was not for me, and the FBI path was over. Graduation was only months away, and now I had to start interviewing for a job in the last career that I ever wanted to pursue. I was devastated.

Shortly after this discouraging episode, President Jimmy Carter announced that the United States would be boycotting the 1980 Moscow Olympics. WHAT? Another crushing blow. Was my swimming career now over and my vocation accounting? Unbelievable. What a mess. The band Third Day has a song, "Keep on Shinin'," which sums up how I was feeling in that moment. They sing about the challenge of having faith in the long run, after we've been bruised and battered, and our dreams shattered, and our best-laid plans are now scattered all over the place. Exactly how I was feeling right now because my dreams were lying in a big heap on the floor. No Olympics, no wildlife management, and I was going to be an accountant.

I was definitely having a tough time being able to see how God's hand was directing all of what I thought was a complete mess. At this point, my dreams were shattered and it was so difficult for me to see that God's plans were much bigger than I could have ever thought possible. It's not that I wasn't capable of dreaming big, I was. The problem was my life was shifting so quickly and I thought my plan was a good one, which included big goals. Little did I know, God's path was going to be so much better. God was asking me to grow in my faith and trust Him, right now.

Psalm 139 verses 13–16 assure us that God has a plan for our lives:

"You made all the delicate, inner parts of my body and knit me together in my mother's womb. Thank you for making me so wonderfully complex! Your workmanship is marvelous – and how well

I know it. You watched me as I was being formed in the utter seclusion, as I was woven together in the dark of the womb. You saw me before I was born. Every day of my life was recorded in your book. Every moment was laid out before a single day had passed" (NLT).

So easy to forget God when "our plans" aren't going the way we hoped. Looking back over a marathon swimming career that lasted thirteen summers after college, it is now easy to see how public accounting was the perfect career for me. Very few other professions would have allowed me to take two to three months off each summer to train and race around the world, competing in the sport that I loved.

Had everything gone perfectly in "my plan," I would have retired from swimming after the Olympics. At the time, I had fallen away from God and forgotten how much He truly loved me and was directing my life, even while my back was turned away from Him.

Ron and I would remain close friends until his passing in 2009. He was a Renaissance man of true inspiration; he continued to compete into his eighties and learned classical Spanish guitar in his seventies. He brought out my athletic potential in ways that other coaches may not have been able to do. I love this quote from his book:

"The real environment of greatness in sport is one of wondrous awareness, of exciting new challenges, constant new motivational techniques and the discipline to do things you only imagined would be possible. You might say the catalyst for super-achievement is knowing that you are doing something that only very few—if any—other human beings have ever tried before. Paradoxically, this environment is built out of daring risks and adventure. Talk about the supreme paradox. Thomas Edison had a sign in his lab, visible for all to see, 'There aren't any rules around here; we are trying to accomplish something."

Thank you, Ron, for the amazing gift you were to countless athletes and everyone who was fortunate enough to know you. Your book is a fine legacy, inspiring generations to come. Because of you, your teachings, and friendships, we all achieved more than we ever thought possible, and had a blast doing it together. I miss you, Ron.

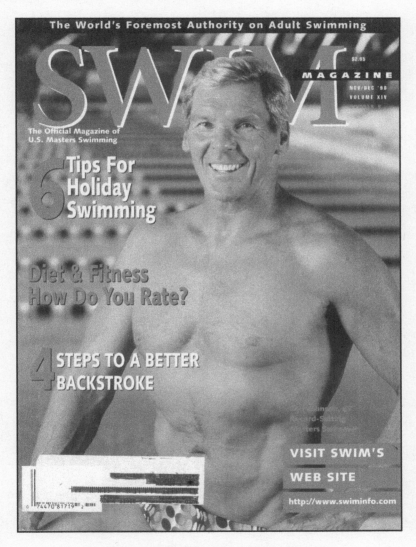

Ron "the Rock" Johnson at age sixty-nine!
Photo courtesy of *Swimming World* magazine

Capri–Napoli
1982

Campionato Mondiale Nuoto Gran Fondo

(Long Distance Swimming World Championship)

The World Professional Marathon Swimming Federation (WPMSF) utilized a series of races around the world to determine an annual male and female "professional marathon swimming world champion." There were typically five to ten annual races included in the world championship series.

The Capri to Naples marathon swim across the Bay of Naples started in 1954 and was organized by Lello Barbuto, sports editor for the Naples newspaper *Il Mattino*, and sanctioned by the International Long Distance Swimming Federation (which I had never heard of) and the WPMSF. I had heard about the race from the other swimmers, but everyone had been fairly quiet about who to contact and how to enter with James Kegley and me during our first two years on the marathon swimming circuit. We had been winning several of the races, especially warm-water ones, which this would be. And heck, I wouldn't have wanted us to come race there, either, if I were them.

In 1982, Lello invited me to compete in the July 4 Capri race for the first time, and despite the limited prize money I accepted. Since inception, the race had been dominated by swimmers from Egypt, Syria, Italy, Yugoslavia, and Argentina. Only one American man had ever won the race, John Kinsella in 1978. Three USA women had won, Greta Anderson in 1959, Diana Nyad in 1974, and Tina Bishoff in 1980 and 1981. Not such a good historical showing from Team USA men compared with the North American races.

When I arrived at the Napoli airport, Lello and his sixteen-year-old daughter Roberta were there to greet me. I was exhausted after 20-plus hours of flying from California and very pleased that the Barbutos were there to meet me. Roberta was a godsend as she spoke excellent English, which was important since Lello spoke little, and I spoke no Italian. The June weather was hot and humid and comfortable for me, but not for Lello, who clearly didn't enjoy the heat in his business suit and tie.

We drove through the craziest traffic that I had ever experienced, our chauffer acting like a race-car driver speeding and weaving through cars on the way to the event headquarters. Traffic lights are merely a suggestion on the streets of Naples, and the most brazen drivers gained the advantage. Being in the car witnessing the most bizarre scene of swearing, honking, and gesturing (which I'm sure were not kind) I had ever witnessed, caused me to start feeling the heat, too, and I couldn't wait to be out of the car.

As we drove through the city I couldn't help noticing the devastating destruction of many structures. Roberta told me how the major earthquake in November 1980 had caused horrific damage to the city and loss of lives throughout the region of Campania. The damage was still clearly evident, with scaffolding on numerous buildings. Rebuilding was going to take years.

We finally arrived at the race headquarters, located in a city park across the street from the Bay of Naples and where the race would finish. As I looked out over the bay I was in awe of the huge mountain that dominates the eastern skyline, Mount Vesuvius. Wow, she is impressive and frightening at the same time. Her last eruption was in 1944, but she is still considered one of the most dangerous volcanoes in the world, with 3,000,000 people living in proximity to her power.

Mount Vesuvius is best known for the eruption in AD 79, which unleashed one of the largest volcanic explosions in European history. The towns of Pompeii and Herculaneum, with 15,000 to 20,000 inhabitants, were buried under the ash.

The city of Naples was unlike anywhere that I had ever been— crowded and noisy, and the people seemed to be on edge, "yelling" and enthusiastically gesturing at each other on a regular basis. Having never been to Italy, I wasn't accustomed to the raised voices and hand waving that I was learning are just part of normal conversation. Welcome to Italy.

Naples is where pizza is said to have been invented, and you can see 2,000-year-old ovens in Pompeii that look just like the brick pizza ovens built today. These were probably used to cook flat breads like focaccia, as tomato wasn't added to pizza until the late 1800s. Swimming burns a lot of calories and I was sure looking forward to trying some of their renowned specialty pastas and pizzas.

The Bay of Naples is part of the Tyrrhenian Sea, which stretches along the west coast of Italy from Corsica to the north and Sicily to the south and is a part of the larger Mediterranean Sea. The swimming race would be about 20 miles from the Isle of Capri to the shore of Naples, finishing just west of the beautiful Castel dell'Ovo (Egg Castle).

After a few formalities at the office, and a small amount of expense money to cover meals during the week, the three of us set off across the bay on a hydrofoil ferry boat to Capri. As the huge turbine engines started to roar, the boat picked up speed and was lifted out of the water by the foils under the hull. The trip from Mergellina Marina to Marina Grande in Capri took less than 40 minutes, as the boat cruised along at speeds above 30 miles per hour. This would be the same route that I would swim in a few days for 7 hours or so, depending on weather conditions.

The bay was beautiful, with the mountains to the east, the Amalfi coastline and Capri to the south, and the islands of Ischia and Procida covering the northwestern edge. As we approached the Isle of Capri, I could see the craggy and rocky shoreline with incredible limestone cliffs rising out of the sea for over 1,000 feet. The sheer walls a tapestry of slate, sepia, and sand colors, and rising into a mountain peak of 1,900 feet at the Monte Solaro summit.

As the ferry pulled into the picturesque Marina Grande harbor I could easily tell we were not in Naples anymore. Tourists from all over the world were bustling about the harbor, queuing up at Motoscafisti for boat rides to the famous "Grotto Azzurra" (Blue Grotto) or around the island tours. The locals quickly jumped on the *Funiculare* (tram), which lifts passengers from the harbor to the Capri Piazza, small red buses, or sped away on their mopeds.

The bustling harbor was filled with small fishing boats painted in vibrant yellows and blues, rigged with netting and gear, along with the larger personal yachts, ferry boats, and island tour boats. All this set against the backdrop of historic residences, villas, and hotels was stunning and I loved the feelings and aromas. Growing up boating in Florida, the smells wafting from fishing and boat fumes in the marina made me feel right at home. Small cafes and tourist shops surrounded the harbor and everyone seemed to be enjoying themselves—what a different vibe than in Naples.

At the end of the harbor dock taxis were waiting to take us up to the top of the island. These were the most unique-looking convertible cars I had ever seen. They had blue-and-white or red-and-white striped fabric awning canopies that served as the car's "roof," and the two bench seats all faced each other—so unique. The drive took us up a very narrow winding stone streets lined with rock walls. These small roads had originally been built for small wagons and now there was just enough room for two cars to slowly maneuver past one another with great care. (Definitely not a time to have your elbow hanging out of the window.)

There are no cars allowed in the Capri city center and we walked from the taxi stand through the historic piazza and down narrow cobblestoned pathways to my hotel, La Rezidenza. After checking in to the hotel, Lello and Roberta told me about the prerace meeting and then had to go back to Naples. Even though I was sad to see them leave I had learned a lot about the race history and seen enough of Capri to know that I was glad to have come. It is truly a magical place.

At night, people wander around the streets to visit, shop, dine, and finish off the evening with a glass of wine or gelato. I quickly discovered the most amazing gelato I've ever tasted at the Buonocore Gelateria, just down from the piazza. Enjoying a just-baked waffle cone slathered with freshly made *strachiatella* (chocolate chip) gelato every day got me race ready.

In the mornings the swimmers who had already arrived for the race gathered for an ocean training swim together, and I looked forward to this. The only problem was that I couldn't sleep due to the time change and was waking up at around noon every day, missing the swim. This was not the best way to prepare for the race in a few days. I knew that the most important thing was to get enough sleep, rest, and fuel. So I focused on sleeping when I could, swimming in the sea to acclimate to the water conditions, and eating the delicious foods of Capri.

On one afternoon swim I was stung on my left forearm by the tentacles of either a Portuguese man o' war or poisonous jellyfish. I had been stung many times by jellyfish in other ocean races and in training, but nothing like this. The sting made me immediately nauseous and I had to leave the water right away and lie down. My arm was on fire with the poison injections from the tentacles that had wrapped around my arm three times. The only thing that I knew to do was rub gel from aloe vera leaves on the wound. Thankfully these succulents grew abundantly on the island. Hopefully this would be the only incident, as I would never be able to finish a marathon swimming race after such a sting.

Besides this one unfortunate incident, swimming in the waters around Capri is the most breathtaking experience for an open water swimmer. The water is sapphire blue with visibility that seems infinite. The beaches are made up of rocks smoothed by years of pounding waves, along with rounded pieces of ancient terra cotta pottery; there is no sand to murky the water.

Swimming from the Marina Grande beach, north along the limestone cliffs, there are times when I felt like I was flying. Huge boulders that had fallen down from the mountain would suddenly rise up in front of me and there would only be two feet between the rock and my body. Moving over the rock made me feel like I was swimming fast and then unexpectedly the rock would stop, and I would be looking into the dark, blue abyss, giving this unusual feeling of "flying." The sheer limestone cliffs tower over 1,000 feet above the sea and continue down into what seems like infinite depths of water as I look down into nothingness; here be sea monsters! I hoped not. What an incredible place to be. I wonder what the apostle Paul would have thought about Capri as he sailed past on his way to Rome via the port of Puteoli (modern-day city of Pozzuoli), located on the northwest section of the Bay of Naples. He would have seen what Mount Vesuvius looked like before the eruption that was about to come.

One day I did get up early enough to swim with the other athletes, and we swam 1½ miles (about 30 minutes) down to the famous Blue Grotto. Along the way I tasted sweet, fresh water coming out of the cliffs and stopped to investigate. There was a narrow passage in the rocks that I squeezed through, and inside was a small cave with a fresh-water spring. The opening I entered through had the rusty remnants of an old iron gate to keep people out, and there was another small opening at the top of the cave. Back outside I noticed that there was a very narrow pathway coming down the side of the sheer cliff, and I could only imagine slaves during Roman rule navigating down this precipitous path to fetch precious fresh water for their island rulers. From AD 27 to his death in AD 37, the Roman emperor Tiberius governed the empire from Capri and built Villa Jovis, whose extensive ruins are still standing today for easy exploration and stunning, unobstructed views of the Amalfi Coast and surrounding seas.

Continuing on our journey, we swam through the small opening into the Blue Grotto, and once inside I was amazed by the beauty of the light filtering through the emerald-blue water and shimmering and dancing shadows of azure hues all over the walls of the large grotto. Such a beautiful sight, something I could only imagine in a dream, or what heaven may look like.

The sunlight primarily enters the cavern through a large opening underneath the water, where it reflects off the white sandy bottom. As we swam, the disturbed waters around our bodies turned into a glistening silver, something I had never experienced before. Another truly magical Capri moment and a must-do experience for anyone visiting the island.

The prerace meeting arrived before I knew it, and after listening to the formalities of the competition there was a drawing for each swimmer's boat pilot. Having an experienced boat pilot in the open sea would be key for me to finish well. When my name was called, the boat pilot selected for me was Giuseppe "Peppino" Vuotto. Peppino had grown up on Capri and was a Blue Grotto and island tour boat pilot with the Motoscafisti group, just like his father, and owned his own boat. Peppino was about ten years older than me and spoke at least five languages that he used daily with the island's international tourists. He reminded me of the American actor Robert Conrad with his rugged seafaring look, dark-brown hair, blue eyes, and bronze skin from working in the sun every day. His boat was about 25 feet long with a center console and inboard engine. The propeller was underneath the boat, which made it very safe for escorting swimmers.

Peppino and I got along well immediately, and I really liked that he knew the local sea so well and was also an avid fisherman. He also had experience escorting swimmers in prior years' events and made me feel very confident for the competition. Despite never helping in a marathon swim before, Roberta Barbuto agreed to help feed and communicate with me about what would be happening during the crossing. I felt that we made an excellent team and looked forward to the race.

When I arrived at Marina Grande on race morning I was surprised to see the beach packed with fans, media, dignitaries, politicians, prior race winners, and athletes. Within a few minutes of being surrounded by all of the commotion, I quickly retreated to Peppino's boat, which was a few hundred feet away from the beach, in the harbor, for a little peace before the race. Peppino, Roberta, and I went over the feeding schedule and made sure everything was ready for the day. Peppino's nine-year-old daughter Alvina joined us, too, for the experience.

All of the swimmers were required to be at the beach and getting ready 30 minutes before the start, and for photographs. Roberta rubbed the lanolin around my neck and under my arms to protect me from salt-water chafing and then had to leave to board Peppino's boat.

The water was around 80 degrees and the air still; it was going to be a hot and humid day. With no wind the sea was glassy and the only disturbance were waves caused by the ferry and race escort boats. Ideal racing conditions.

Twenty-three competitors from twelve countries were on the beach this morning, hoping to complete the challenge of crossing the Bay of Naples and win the world championship race. There is always so much that can go wrong over 7 or more hours and I was my usual nervous self at the start. After a few speeches from the officials and dignitaries we entered the water and waited for the start. I had a few minutes before the starter's pistol would sound and swam around the start line to loosen up and keep my nerves in check.

This was the beginning of my third summer on the professional marathon swimming racing circuit and I knew most of the other athletes. Claudio Plit from Argentina was going to be the biggest challenge, as he had won this marathon the last three years and competed five times in the race since 1973. Last year's race was shortened and swum in the Naples harbor due to extremely rough conditions. The seas were too dangerous for the smaller escort boats. Nothing like this year's conditions.

There were also new faces from Italy, Egypt, Syria, and Yugoslavia that I had not competed against and knew from training swims that they were fast swimmers. Today my race strategy was to set an early fast pace and see how everyone else would respond.

The starter's pistol finally sounded and we took off out into the sea. The usual chaos of the swimmer, official, media, and spectator boats all wanting to be in the same location ensued. I had seen Peppino's boat from the beach and headed directly for him, ignoring all the mad splashing around me.

Peppino and I had practiced during the week the pace that I wanted to swim, how rapidly we would feed, and my location alongside the boat. The boat was right where I wanted it on my left side and near the midpoint of the hull. I immediately established a fast rhythm of 84 strokes per minute and could easily see Roberta and any messages she might write on the dry erase board.

Within minutes of swimming away from the beach, the water turned a deep sapphire blue and I could see nothing below me but darkness, feeling like a bottomless pit. Visibility was over 200 feet but there was nothing to see and I was glad to have the nearness of the boat. Peppino had assured me that there were no big sharks "this time of year." Comforting.

My rapid early pace brought me swiftly to the lead and I concentrated on nothing but breathing and pushing my stroke rate, exerting to be on the edge of my aerobic threshold, the place where there is enough blood oxygen and energy stores from my liver and muscles to sustain the energy needed by my muscles at this effort level. If I pushed too hard, blood lactate would be produced at high levels, creating an anaerobic condition, and I would have to slow down until swimming aerobically again. I felt great and pushed the pace, knowing that I was having a good day and swimming fast. Stroke, stroke, breathe, stroke, stroke, breathe... holding 84 strokes a minute.

I focused on swimming as close to the boat as possible to take advantage of the "V-shaped" hull breaking through the waves. There is a "sweet spot" when swimming next to boats that are long enough, located about halfway down the hull. The bow breaks through the waves, making the water calmer for the swimmer, and the boat's midpoint is away from the exhaust, typically at the stern. The only downside of swimming so close was that waves moved the boat from time to time, causing my left hand to whack a small metal bilge pump plate midway up the hull. A few times wasn't a problem, but over the day, after hitting this uneven metal dozens of times, a painful wound opened up. Glad there were no big sharks around.

Out in the open sea there was nothing but the boat and blue abyss underneath me now. Then out of nowhere I was surrounded by a school of small silver fish, about 6 inches long. There were thousands of them, as far as I could see horizontally and vertically. They made room for me within their school as if I was one of them. Just as my hand was about to enter the water and would seemingly hit a small fish, they would move away just enough; we were swimming together in an amazing dance. What a breathtaking experience. I tried to take it all in while staying focused on my commitment to push the pace as fast as I could.

Music was part of every race that I did and seemed to be even more prevalent when I felt good. Typically, the lyrics of a song I had heard hundreds of times would play over and over. Today I felt so good that I imagined myself a flying fish skimming over the top of the water with Lynyrd Skynyrd's "Free Bird" guitar solo blasting through my head. I was flying high, just like the free bird. Pushing, pushing, pushing...

Roberta and Peppino were a great team, and after a few hours they told me not to worry about the other swimmers and to just keep going. We had opened up a big lead. The water was warm and now I was hot and tired, and my mouth raw from the high salt levels of the Mediterranean. This sea has one of the highest salinity levels of any open body of water due to being almost completely closed off to the larger oceans, along with a high degree of evaporation. Swimming in high-salinity water makes the swimmer's body more buoyant and therefore faster. The downside is the excessive salt causes your mouth and tongue to swell, and if not careful with lubricants, bad skin chafing can result.

Roberta feeding me during the race with very calm sea
Photo courtesy of *Il Mattino*, Napoli, Italy

After 4 hours I was still swimming strongly and fast, and knew that
we had a good finish in store if I could continue the pace. The entry to
the finish area was clearly marked by a big buoy near Castel dell'Ovo, and
it was good to know exactly where we were going; the bad news was the
castle is so big we could see it from a long ways away and it felt like forever
to move closer. At each 20-minute feeding, it seemed as though we had
made no progress toward the towering structure, so I quit looking at the
castle and just focused on Roberta, Peppino, and the side of the boat.

Nearing the finish of the race swimming by Castel dell'Ovo,
Mount Vesuvius in background

As we approached the Naples harbor the water turned from azure blue to emerald green, and then we started to see more garbage from the land. As we continued closer, the water lost the pristine visibility of Capri and turned grey and foul-smelling. (At the time of this race, the Bay of Naples was heavily polluted. Since then, a major successful cleanup effort was undertaken by the communities surrounding the bay to improve these waters. We "fish" both with and without gills are grateful.)

Closer and closer we came to the final touch pad and I continued to push my pace, keep my stroke rate above 80 strokes a minute, and focus only on the next 20 minutes. Before I knew it we were in the finish chute, completing the last 1,000 meters along the Naples waterfront promenade and past the race headquarters building where I was first introduced to this amazing race, wonderful people, and natural beauty.

When I breathed to my right I could see thousands of spectators watching along the promenade, cheering and waving Italian flags. Peppino expertly guided me to the race finish pad, which I touched with joy and relief. I swam over to thank Peppino, Roberta, and Alvina; we were all crying with joy. Then I was greeted on the dock by Lello—he was so happy! Our team of Peppino, Roberta, and me had made history that day with a new record of 6 hours and 35 minutes, beating the old record set in 1974 by more than 30 minutes. We were all thrilled, and it was very fitting for an American to win on the Fourth of July! Go USA!

Big smiles with Peppino Vuotto after the marathon finished

Plit finished second about 25 minutes back and 5 minutes faster than the old record. A great day for Claudio. Nineteen of the twenty-three swimmers were able to conquer the Bay of Naples today.

Lello had me get into an ambulance for a checkup; just a short drive to the medical facilities, about ½ mile away at the race headquarters. I thought nothing of it until the ambulance driver decided that he was in a Formula One race car and we sped off as fast as the vehicle could go. The roadway was closed but I still felt my life was in danger; it was one of the scariest 30 seconds of my life. The newspaper headlines flashed through my mind: "Capri–Napoli winner killed in freak ambulance accident."

There is such relief after finishing a marathon swim—relief from the pain that has been nagging your back and shoulders for hours, relief to have finished an accomplishment that most people couldn't fathom attempting, and when winning, financial relief to pay for travel and living expenses.

Peppino had to go back to Capri and was already heading home. Roberta caught up with me and I let her know that I was starving. Along with her younger brother Paolo, we headed across the street to the marina restaurant by the castle. No matter what food I would have eaten in that moment, the cantaloupe wrapped with prosciutto was the most wonderful delicacy I had ever had—cold, sweet, juicy melon, matched with the salty meat was the perfect combination. We also had fresh, home-made pasta that melted in my mouth. What a wonderful ending to an amazing day.

The next day Roberta came by my hotel and asked that I come to the race headquarters and bring the same swimwear I raced in. I thought this was a bit odd, but she told me that the *Il Mattino* newspaper wanted to take a few more pictures at the finish area. There was a photographer there with long blond hair who let us know what he wanted. The finish pad was still set up and I swam in several times and lifted my arms in victory, similar to the day before but without all the emotion. Hard to replicate real emotion like that. I later learned that the photographer from the sponsoring newspaper missed the finish, as no one had ever swum under 7 hours and he thought he had a lot of time. I'm glad not to have witnessed the meeting between Lello and the photographer when Lello found out what happened.

Peppino came back to Naples the next day for the awards ceremony, which was held on a big, new ferry boat. There were a lot of dignitaries and speeches, and after receiving my awards we both grew antsy and started exploring the bowels of this special vessel. We spent hours discovering the intricacies of the state-of-the-art boat, from the engine room to the pilothouse. It was a highlight of the day.

When we got back to the hotel Italy was playing Brazil in the World

Cup soccer tournament. I was too tired to stay up and went to bed, and Peppino went out to watch the match. What seemed to be the middle of the night, I was awakened by honking horns and yelling; I went to the window to see what was happening. I was shocked to see the streets packed wall to wall with people and cars, and everyone waving huge Italian flags. Italy had won 3 to 2 over Brazil; this was emotional jubilation like I've never seen before. Men crying and carrying on with faces of disbelief. Growing up watching SEC football I had seen fanatical sports fans, but this was another whole level of emotion. The Napolitano partied through the night and it wasn't even the finals yet. That's what I call passionate supporters!

The journey to Italy had been much more than I expected and worth the effort to come from California. New friendships were formed that last to this day. The race record held for 30 years, until Trent Grimsey from Australia set a new record of 6 hours and 29 minutes in 2012. We will call that a good run.

Lello Barbuto continued to host the race until 1993, when he suddenly and sadly passed away. New organizers revived the tradition in 2003 and the race continues today under the guidance of the organizing committee president, Luciano Cotena. Lello's son Paulo Barbuto is now the sports editor of the *Il Mattino*, and his sister Roberta lives in Florida. Peppino retired from the Motoscafisti boat group and still fishes regularly in the waters of Capri.

COACH CHARLES "RED" SILVIA

When Coach Sam Freas introduced me to Coach Silvia (Coach) before my first marathon swim in 1980, I didn't realize he would be the most important open water swimming coach I would ever meet. When he was younger he had bright-red hair; hence his nickname of "Red." Coach still had a beautiful head of hair, now all white.

When I met Coach he had recently retired from coaching the Springfield College swim team and was running a summer camp and swimming school in Springfield, Massachusetts, with his wife Ruthie, daughter Susan, and son-in-law David. Sam had attended Springfield College and swam on the swim team under Coach.

Coach Charles Silvia
Photo courtesy of Diddo Clark

Coach's knowledge of anatomy and physics and how the swimming strokes impacted each aspect of the human body was amazing. When I had shoulder problems he knew immediately why and helped me to correct my stroke and alleviate the problem. When you are swimming races lasting 7 hours and more, at 80 strokes a minute (adds up to more than 30,000 arm rotations), having an efficient and anatomically correct stroke is crucial to success and longevity in the sport.

I had no idea of what a great coach Sam had introduced me to and found out later some of his credentials included:

- Developing 50 college swim coaches
- Swimmers setting 14 world records and winning 2 Olympic gold medals
- His swimmer Dr. David Hart set a world-record English Channel crossing in 1972
- President and board chair of the International Swimming Hall of Fame
- Application of Newtonian laws of propulsion to swimming
- Authored one of the first lifesaving books and was the first to endorse mouth-to-mouth insufflations (blowing air into the lungs)

Spending a lot of time with Coach between 1980 and 1992, I learned so much about anatomically correct swimming, efficient stroke technique, and acclimating to cold water. There was no other coach who taught me more about open water swimming and training, and I was very blessed to have ever met him.

Everything that he taught me was so simple and well thought out: "swing and turn" (rotating your torso and swinging your arms), "let your stroke carry you" (not forcing or muscling), and "swim within yourself" (don't try to be someone else). Thoughts that I would remember and carry with me during my races; I had a lot of time to think during 8-hour swims.

In 1984, I suffered an extreme case of bicipital tendonitis and had to stop swimming for six weeks in April and May. Coach quickly analyzed the situation and we corrected my flawed stroke technique. One of his points of emphasis was to "Explore the Big Four":

1. Inertial shoulder girdle elevation and upward scapular rotation
2. Shoulder joint medial rotation and elbow joint flexion
3. Shoulder joint abduction and downward scapular rotation
4. Inertial round off and release (rotating your torso upward and allowing your hand to easily exit the water)

Using anatomically correct language is how Coach communicated with all ages of swimmers until they understood what he was talking about. Observing six-year-olds at his swim camp perform and explain "ankle flexion" was a hoot. He was really brilliant, and thankfully I was able to tap into just a small piece of his knowledge to help my marathon swimming career.

In 1986, I was invited by Dave McGillivray to become the first person to try to swim from Nantucket to Cape Cod. Dave's idea was that the crossing would coincide with the September Cape Cod Ironman Triathlon going on at the same moment. Coach liked the idea. He had a friend, Ron Kramer, in the area with a boat; he who would help us navigate the crossing.

We put together a support team of Coach, Ron, David and Susan Lang, and Don Megerle, the Tufts University head swim coach. Ron did a great job of interpreting the tide charts for that day and laying out our planned course.

The distance across Nantucket Sound to Craigville Beach would be about 24 miles. We knew that there would be lots of current to deal with as well as ocean waves, and hoped that we would be able to complete the swim in 8 hours or less by averaging my usual speed of 3 miles per hour. The water temp of near 70 degrees would not typically be an issue for me. Of course Dave, being the ultimate sports promoter, wanted us to try to finish around the same time as the triathlon winners would be crossing the finish line. Mother Nature was in charge, and would end up having her way with us.

After spending the night in Nantucket we started the crossing on a small beach just to the west of the harbor entrance at around 9 a.m. The day was cloudy with little wind and the crew was very excited. Knowing it was going to be a long day and not a race, I was calm and asked the crew to keep their excitement to a "medium level of enthusiasm." They thought this was really funny but I did not. Nothing is more annoying than emotional intensity from my support crew when none is needed during an endurance event. Encouragement, yes; overly enthusiastic, no.

Coach Don Megerle, head swimming coach, Tufts University

What I was thrilled the most about this day was to be swimming an event with Coach in the boat. Because of Coach's summer camp schedule, he had only been able to see one other marathon swimming event of mine when I attempted to cross the English Channel in 1985. I was always honored to be around him.

The crossing ended up being much more challenging than any of us would have thought. There are a lot of shoals in Nantucket Sound and when the moving water reaches an area with a shallower depth, the speed of the current increases to allow the same volume of water to move past in the same amount of time. These areas of increased current pushed us much farther east into the Atlantic Ocean than we had planned.

Being farther to the east normally would not have been a big deal, and we could have touched Cape Cod anywhere to complete the swim. However, we had agreed with Dave that I would finish at Craigville Beach where the triathlon was finishing, which was now several miles west of us, and the tide was running out to the east. This was a problem as I was forced to swim directly against the current, parallel to the Cape Cod beaches, and the sun was going down.

None of us had anticipated that the crossing would take so long that I would be swimming in the dark. Swimming in an ocean where there are known to be sharks is one thing for me to handle during the day. Swimming in an ocean at night where there are known to be sharks was now freaking me out. What turned out to be a good idea was now a bad one as far as I was concerned. I did the only thing that I knew to do and prayed, *"Lord, I'm really scared, please bring me home safely."*

Why we didn't think to have me just swim into shore at the closest point, record the crossing time, and then all ride calmly in the boat over to Craigville Beach, I really don't know. But we committed to Dave that we would finish at Craigville Beach, and now hour after excruciating hour I swam against the current until finally finishing the crossing 12 hours and 1 minute after starting. It was the longest swim that I had ever done, and more than 4 hours after the triathlon winners. Nice idea.

Coach seemed more relieved than happy, and I was, too. David and Susan's young children met me on the shore and we walked to the triathlon finish banner together. Dave was very excited to see me cross the "finish line."

Crossing the Ironman finish line after swimming 12 hours
from Nantucket to Craigville Beach, Cape Cod
Photo courtesy of Dave McGillivray

There are special people in an athlete's journey who really make the difference between success and having an "also swum" career; Coach Silvia was one of those people for me, and many other athletes. There are not enough ways to express my gratitude to him for his help during my swimming career; his years of advice were key to both my victories and sport longevity. When I was inducted into the International Swimming Hall of Fame in 2010, I prayed that Coach Silvia was looking down from heaven, smiling and feeling proud. It wouldn't have happened without him.

THE ENGLISH CHANNEL
1985

"Nothing great is easy"
—Captain Matthew Webb

D uring my first five years of marathon swimming, I had competed in 32 international races, 1 solo swim, and had won 5 World Professional Marathon Swimming Federation world championships. I had accomplished much more in the world of open water swimming than I ever imagined would have happened after starting the sport in 1980.

My "summer job" of marathon swimming had been very successful so far and I continued to enjoy the journey of training hard, traveling, catching up with friends, making new friends around the world, and most of all racing (winning was also a big part of the joy). I was a CPA during this time with Kenneth Leventhal in Newport Beach, California, and then moved to the San Francisco Bay Area in 1982, where I worked for Ernst & Whinney (now Ernst & Young) in their San Jose and San Francisco offices. Life was good and I received my share of media exposure for a sport that wasn't well known.

When I would meet someone new and the topic of marathon swimming would come up, they would be genuinely interested in learning about the sport and what it was I did. As soon as they understood that the races were typically in the ocean or lakes and were longer than 20 miles, they couldn't wait to ask "their" question. Once they had their question in mind it didn't matter how many races I had won or world championships earned, they had to ask, "Have you ever swum the English Channel?" When I answered, "No," there would be an awkward pause and the conversation would change as they didn't want to offend me now that they knew I wasn't a "real marathon swimmer," or at least not a very good one. I found this intriguing and a good lesson in human behavior, how we often form conclusions without waiting to understand the true scope of what we are hearing. Knowing that this type of interaction would continue, I knew that one day I would need to add a Channel crossing to my swimming resume. Especially for casual cocktail conversation.

The English Channel is a distance of 21 miles from the beach at the base of the beautiful white cliffs of Dover, England, eastward across the busiest shipping channel in the world to Cap Gris-Nez (Cape Gray Nose), France. The distance isn't that long compared to other marathon swims I competed in, but the Channel has wicked currents caused by extreme changes between high and low tide, typically strong winds, choppy conditions, and cold-water temperatures of around 60 degrees.

On August 25, 1875, the United Kingdom's Captain Matthew Webb captured worldwide attention when he became the first person to successfully cross the English Channel unaided in 21 hours and 45 minutes. Captain Webb received immediate national and international fame for a feat most thought to be humanly impossible, and open water marathon swimming events were born. Over the next eight years, Webb completed many swimming challenges and stunts like floating in a tank of water for 128 hours. He was a great swimmer who in the end overestimated his abilities, when he tragically died trying to swim the Whirlpool Rapids of the Niagara River below Niagara Falls, New York. His older brother Thomas dedicated a memorial in Captain Webb's hometown Dawley, Telford, which reads, "Nothing great is easy."

Coach Silvia was going to be taking a swimmer across the Channel in August of 1985 and I decided that it would be a good time to add an

English Channel crossing to my swimming accomplishments. At least a successful crossing would add a positive comment during cocktail conversation about marathon swimming.

Phillip Rush from New Zealand, his coach Tony Keenan, and I took the redeye flight from New York City to London and arrived in Folkestone, England, on August 7. We were greeted with perfect English Channel weather of heavy wind and rain as if the elements were challenging us right from the start. Philip was there to try a nearly impossible double or triple crossing of the Channel and I was there for a hard enough one-way crossing. I knew that if everything went just right it might be possible for me to break the England to France record of 7 hours and 40 minutes set by Penny Dean in 1978.

There are three main environmental factors that affect a successful English Channel crossing: tides, wind, and water temperature. The tides along the eastern coast of Great Britain are tremendous, with a difference between low tide and high tide of greater than 7 meters (23 feet). This is caused by both the relatively shallow European continental shelf that extends around this area along with the narrowing of the lands between Great Britain and France, creating a funnel that causes the water to squeeze between these two land masses. An enormous amount of water has to move in one direction approximately every 6 hours, and when the water gets squeezed coming through the narrow channel, it picks up speed.

Because these moon and sun cycles are predictable and known years in advance, swimmers trying to cross the Channel plan their swims when the difference between high tide and low tide is the smallest; these time periods are called neap tides, when the current moves the slowest. When the difference between high and low tides is the greatest the current runs fastest and these periods of time are called spring tides. Each of these segments of time periods covers almost two weeks. There have been successful channel crossings during spring tides and the boat captain and swimmer both know that they will be swept farther north and south as the current moves swiftly through the Channel. Traveling farther north and south creates more risk when you are trying to swim from west to east, as you never know where you will make landfall.

With the tide chart known well in advance, channel swimmers and their captains plan their crossings in the months when the water is typically warmest and calmest, during July, August, and September. The unknowns continue to be wind and water temperature. There is a small group of certified channel boat captains whom swimmers need to book for a crossing escort; only they have permission from the English Channel Swimming Association as well as the French and British coast guards. Each captain typically has a first, second, third, etc. position for swimmers during specific neap tide periods. If you miss your window of opportunity due to bad weather, you may miss your chance to swim that year or end up in a third or fourth position during the next neap tide two weeks later, which can be very frustrating.

Philip and I had competed in *Les Quatorze Miles de Paspebiac* (the 14 miles of Paspebiac) in Quebec the weekend before our arrival and were both a bit tired, but we immediately got into the daily routine of training in the cold English Channel waters. Depending on the weather, we either trained in Dover Harbor or at the Folkestone beach. Growing up boating I was on the water many days in Florida and had been to many marinas all around the state. However, I had never seen a scene like Folkestone Harbor at low tide with all the boats resting on the muddy bottom. What a surprise. It also let me know how severe the currents were going to be and something to be taken extremely seriously.

My preparation for the summer of racing was the best that I had experienced and I was very confident in my preparation. I lived in San Francisco at this time and regularly trained in Aquatic Park Cove. This swimming area is located in San Francisco Bay at the end of the Hyde Street Cable Car line—what an iconic place to train. I was a member of the South End Rowing Club, where a group of committed open water swimmers braved the bay's cold temperatures year round. I was definitely a more fair-weather open water swimmer and waited for the water temperature to near 60 degrees before getting in. The comradery and encouragement of the club members during my preparation swims boosted my resolve during the long hours of training. Watching men and women more than twice my age swimming in the cold bay water year round was very inspiring. Their zeal for open water swimming gave me additional motivation to dedicate my channel swim to others.

The South End Rowing Club was founded in 1873 and is one of the oldest athletic clubs west of the Mississippi—one of the oldest institutions in San Francisco. Training in the cove and having the historic clubhouse next to the rival Dolphin Club was always something to which I looked forward. Swimming with views of Ghirardelli Square, San Francisco Maritime Museum, Golden Gate Bridge, Alcatraz Island, and Mount Tamalpais was a magical experience. The daily fog and wind rolling in from the Pacific Ocean made the venue cold and choppy, and a perfect place to acclimate for the English Channel chill.

My job as a certified public accountant with Ernst & Whinney (now known as Ernst & Young) was on the thirtieth floor of the Bank of America building on California Street. From our offices you could see the Golden Gate and Bay Bridges, Coit Tower, and a long southerly view to China Camp and Hunters Point near the San Francisco airport. Each day either during my lunch break or after work, I would walk several blocks to the San Francisco Olympic Club on Post Street for pool training.

The Olympic Club, established on May 6, 1860, is the oldest athletic club in the United States and has the most beautiful indoor pool I've ever seen. The club has one of the best masters swimming groups in the world and there was almost always someone in the pool to train alongside with morning, noon, or night. At this time the club was men only, and training alongside teammates who were in their sixties, seventies, and eighties was both humbling and motivating. The club's board of directors generously voted to help financially support my English Channel quest and I will be forever grateful.

After the tax busy season was over I ramped up my training at both the Aquatic Park cove and the Olympic Club pool until leaving for Mission Viejo in the third week of May. The Mission Viejo Nadadores were coached by the International Swimming Hall of Fame coach Mark Schubert at this time. The Nadadores were the perennial USA national championship team with many Olympic gold medalists, world and American record holders, and national champions on the team. I had the pleasure of training with Mark and the Nadadores since 1976 and looked forward to the pool, Lake Mission Viejo, and Laguna Beach workouts each summer break. My Mission Viejo "family," Dick and Michelle Africano, along with their children Lynn, Mark, Brad, and Dawn, were always waiting for my summer training visit, to make me feel at home and a part of their loving family. An athlete could not ask for more.

While working full time, a typical training day would be one workout a day of 6,000–7,000 meters (about 4 miles) and 30,000 to 40,000 meters each week (18 to 25 miles). Once I started my summer break and moved to Mission Viejo, the distance and intensity would dramatically increase to 15,000–20,000 meters per day (9 to 12 miles) and up to 90,000 meters each week (55 miles). Training swims in either Lake Mission Viejo or the Pacific Ocean (typically at Laguna Beach) ranged between 2½ and 3 hours, and were necessary to really prepare me for the 1985 marathon circuit of 4 races over four consecutive weekends, a big challenge. Atlantic City, July 14 – 23 miles; Lac Memphremagog, July 21 – 26 miles; Lac St. Jean double crossing, July 27 &28 – 40 miles; and Paspebiac, August 4 – 16 miles. After all of this, I would travel to England for the Channel crossing.

The summer of 1985, I trained faster than I ever had in my life, and I was almost twenty-eight years old; it was a good sign of what was to come. For shorter distances in the pool I was consistently holding 1 minute and 5 seconds or better for every 100 meters (100 meters equal two lengths of a 50-meter pool, the same as the Olympic pool length). For long pool-training swims of distances over 1,000 meters I was consistently holding 1 minute 10 seconds. My pool times were very fast for a marathon swimmer and historically for me. By the end of my preparation time in Mission Viejo, I knew I was ready for the summer.

With the exception of my abandonment of the Lac St. Jean double crossing, I won all of the other races that summer—Atlantic City (23 miles), Lac Memphremagog (26 miles), and Paspebiac (16 miles). Arriving at the Channel, I felt good and looked forward to swimming one more event before the summer was over.

After a few days of training at the Channel the weather turned very bad and I decided to go to London to see some city sights and train in the Hyde Park Serpentine. The Serpentine is a 40-acre lake in the center of the park created in 1730; pretty hard to fathom the age for a simple Florida boy. The lake is beautiful but not the most pristine place that I had ever swum as the swimmers had to share the waters with many ducks and geese. There was a course about 200 meters long for swimming that had chlorine bubblers along the length for sanitizing the water; this was a first for me. (This small lake was selected as the 10-kilometer Olympic swimming venue in the 2012 London Games.)

Being in London for a few days was a good diversion from the constant Channel crossing conversations while training in Dover Harbor. There were many "expert" opinions on the shores of the Channel, even from some who had never swum an open water marathon in cold water.

Although beginning to feel much better, my left shoulder had been hurting for most of the summer from training and racing, which was concerning me a bit. To help loosen the shoulder muscles, I found a heated 50-meter pool to train in, which served as a good recovery workout, and my shoulder began to improve.

After a week in the 62- to 64-degree Serpentine waters I was back in Dover, training in the 60-degree Channel waters. Swimming in salt water has advantages over fresh water, as the salt makes a swimmer much more buoyant and therefore faster. In addition, 60 degrees in salt water doesn't feel nearly as cold as in fresh water, due to the softness of salt water.

The adjustment from the Serpentine back to the Channel was an easy transition, and I focused in on training 1 hour twice a day in either Dover or Folkestone with icy showers only. I had done more cold-water acclimatization over the last three months than ever before, and the water no longer made me shiver during workouts or afterward as my body warmed up. An excellent sign my body had acclimated to these frigid temperatures.

The advantage of solo swims is you only swim when the weather is good, versus open water racing when we line up at the starting line whether the wind and rain are howling or not, or the current is with you or not. The weather was turning nicer; we all looked forward to the next neap tide period and the crossing we had been waiting almost three weeks for now.

Ray and Audrey Scott ran the English Channel Swimming Association at this time and were the consummate hosts to the swimmers who had come from around the world to this small village in Southeast England to try a feat that had only a 10 percent success rate. There have been more than twice as many successful summits of Mount Everest (about 8,300) versus English Channel crossings (about 3,900). Just like climbing Mount Everest, swimming the English Channel was the ultimate athletic achievement for many and their lifelong dream. Sadly, most would not achieve their goal and some would even give their life to the quest. Swimming for many hours in cold water is a dangerous undertaking and has to be approached with the utmost care, preparation, and education, along with an experienced crew prepared to save your life if needed.

Thanks to Coach Silvia, I had learned that one of the most important skills to have while swimming in cold water is the ability to maintain a high heart rate. Swimming while keeping my heart rate elevated allowed my body to generate enough heat to stay warm. Training in cold water acclimated my body to colder temperatures, but once fatigue sets in and my heart rate drops, hypothermia will begin to take over in short order. Unless the athlete can somehow recover and raise the heart rate, their swim will be over. This is the fate of most who come to swim the channel during this period of time.

With Coach Silvia beside the bust of Captain Mathew Webb,
Dover Harbor, Great Britain
Photo courtesy of Diddo Clark

Leading up to the channel crossing, there was much to arrange with
the boat pilot and other swim logistics, such as prerace photos arranged
by Ernst & Whinney and some filming by a videographer we had hired.
After much discussion, Coach Silvia and I decided that instead of being
second on a pilot's list of swimmers we were better off switching boat
captains so that we could be first when the best tides and days to swim
arrived. With this in mind, we met with Captain Mike Oram, who agreed
to be our escort.

Unlike marathon races where I was used to having only one person to
travel with and support me in the boat during the race, the larger escort

boat allowed more people to help and cheer during the swim. The support crew would include Maura Campion (Maura and I were married from 1983 to 1994 and had two children, Kendall and Logan. Kendall was born in 1986 and Logan in 1990), Maura's brother Brian Campion, Bay Area friend Diddo Clark, Coach Silvia, childhood friends Mary Lee Brooks and Kitty Williams from Fort Myers, and our videographer Russell Baxter were also on the boat; we had a big crew to encourage me across.

Swimming the English Channel is an expensive undertaking—airfares, food and lodging for many weeks while waiting for the right day, the escort boat, crossing fees, and incidentals. To help defer some of these costs, Maura and Diddo did a very good job of raising money from friends and family, as well as two tickets from American Airlines, which was very generous. The Olympic Club and Ernst & Whinney also provided financial assistance to achieve the crossing goal. I was overwhelmed by all of the support and proudly hung the Olympic Club banner on our boat. My family, friends, coaches, and teammates from the Olympic Club, the South End Rowing Club, and Mission Viejo were all rooting for a successful crossing, a very awesome feeling.

We finally got the call from our boat pilot Mike Oram that the weather and tide looked like a go for the next day, August 29. I had been feeling better and better in training each day and was ready to go. Sleep before a big swim was usually restless and this night was no different.

When really anxious some nights, I will awake from an anxiety dream of being unable to find the race start while driving around the dirt streets of a foreign city. In these dreams, I usually find the starting location after everyone else has already taken off and quickly jump in after them. After waking on this night, I knew there would be many people waking me up if I overslept in the morning, and tried to get some more rest.

The morning was sunny and calm with fog blanketing the Channel. On the drive to Dover the white cliffs of Cap Blanc-Nez (Cape White Nose) on the French coast rose above the mist, blanketing the water. The calm felt good.

We loaded the boat as quickly as possible and headed out to the beach at the base of the chalky white cliffs of Dover. It was a beautiful, still morning on the Channel and there were a few folks on the beach along with a local photographer who was taking pictures of swimmers setting off. I quickly greased my chafing points and swam the short distance to the beach.

Mike had a zodiac boat with an outboard engine that wasn't working earlier in the week, but he assured me it would be ready by the swim date. It wasn't. The zodiac had to row into the beach with Russell and his camera to film the start.

Besides our support crew and Mike's first mate, the English Channel Swimming Association had assigned us an observer, "Ian," who was responsible for recording the official time and watching to make sure that I followed the rules and was safe throughout the swim.

When the boat gave the signal I started swimming at a good pace and straight out from the beach in the direction the boat was facing. Due to the zodiac engine not working Mike had to wait for the rowers and I was 100 meters in front of the boat by myself before they were able to catch up. I felt great and was swimming at a very strong 84 strokes per minute, a perfect pace. The channel was calm except for wave swells coming from all different directions caused by leftover storms, ferry boat, and hydrofoil crossings. This was definitely the best day I had seen since arriving more than three weeks ago. I started swimming on the starboard side of the boat and Mike moved me over to the port side within the hour so that he could see me better from the wheelhouse. I felt smoother breathing to my left but wasn't bothered by the switch; what I was bothered by was Mike not letting me swim next to the boat, where I needed to be for maximum shelter from the waves, but it wasn't enough to slow me down at all. I was in a good groove and loudly singing in my head "My Jesus Told Me So" by the Marshall Tucker Band.

Near the start of the Channel crossing with White Cliffs of Dover in the background
Photo courtesy of Diddo Clark

Each time I stopped to feed the beautiful cliffs of Dover seemed to tower over the Channel and stay in view forever, and made me feel small and not moving very fast, so I stopped looking at them and focused straight ahead to France. At around the two-hour mark I swallowed some sea water and started vomiting. I was used to this in salt water races and, after stopping for a few seconds, kept going. The joke in marathon swimming when this happens is "at least you didn't get anything on you." Not very funny when it's you getting sick. Amazingly, Captain Mike was oblivious to my stopping and kept moving ahead, leaving me more than 50 meters behind the boat, which can be demoralizing to a swimmer. For me, it was all part of the challenge and I now realized my boat captain talked a better game than he skippered.

The upset stomach didn't bother me much and I kept up a great pace and motivated attitude. There are many things that can and do go wrong during open water marathons. Keeping my attitude in check is the most important goal. Because in every moment of every day, the one thing we get to choose is our attitude; no one else can control this. When cruising along in the open ocean being hit with seaweed, flotsam, jetsam, seasickness, and slimed occasionally by jellyfish (luckily the Channel jelly stings were not fierce), maintaining focus on the goal with a great attitude fuels the competitive fire.

Because the Channel escort boats are much larger than the typically smaller guide boats in the other races, long poles are used to extend the feed cups out to the swimmer. Feedings are more difficult than normal because the feed cups got stuck occasionally in the holders, and the boat is moving up and down in the swells, so feeding from a pole is always a challenge.

Energy from the support crew was very high and everyone was in good spirits. After 5 hours the message was 4½ miles to go and 2 hours to break the record. This was good news, as I was swimming three miles per hour and would break the record at this speed, so I kept pressing the pace. Then with 4 miles to go, the boat relayed the message: 1 hour and 30 minutes to break the record. Mmmmm, something was wrong. To only swim ½ mile in 30 minutes instead of 1½ miles… We were obviously swimming against some current and there was nothing I could do about that except swim my best.

Then with 55 minutes left to break the record, the message to me was 3 miles to go, and I knew breaking the record was doubtful. However, I still felt very strong and kept up a fast pace. Having Coach Silvia on the boat was a treat for me, and in the brief moments I stopped to feed his strong New England-laced voice would ring through with, "You're swimming well, Paul," "You can do it, Paul," and it really meant a lot hearing his encouragement. Having such a big group of supporters on the boat was inspiring, as well, and I loved their enthusiasm.

After the last message Mike must have told the boat the record wasn't happening as I could feel the mood change on the boat, which was quite understandable. For me, I felt very good and didn't feel bad to miss the record. I was having a great marathon achievement; swimming one of the fastest days in my life. The sun started setting and darkness was quickly upon me. I was given a small plastic glowing stick, about 6 inches long and 3/4 inches in diameter that illuminated a fluorescent green light and quickly slid into the backside of my suit so the boat crew would be able to "see me" in the darkness. At least the glow of the light stick.

Swimming at night is a unique experience, as you can see nothing but the small lights of the boat. At the moment, it was very calming for me and frightening for others; there was nothing in the channel to worry about except jellyfish and floating debris, and we had seen very little of either today. While feeling alone in the coal-black night water, I was relaxed and in touch with my soul. At peace.

Suddenly the boat stopped, and I was told to swim ahead to the right by myself, the water depth too shallow for the boat to get closer to shore. I could see nothing in front of me, and now I was scared. My peaceful moments were gone. The zodiac had no working engine to guide me to shore and Mike had not fixed the boat's spotlight to shine on the beach for me to see (another unfulfilled promise), and this put me in serious danger as I swam off into the moonless night. Quickly, no one on the boat could see me in the darkness, there were only stars. As I swam about ¼ mile from the boat I began to make out the cliffs of Cap Gris-Nez; I had made it. Almost.

The scariest part of the day was upon me now. I could hear and feel the waves crashing on the boulders lining the shore of the beach, yet not see the rocks. I was unable to see anything and kept looking at the sky to distinguish the cliffs of the cape against the starlit sky, and listen for the swells breaking on the shore. It was a slow process of feeling my way between the rocks without being pounded against them and cut by sharp edges or barnacles. My hands finally touched the uneven, rock-strewn bottom and I gingerly walked upon the beach. The boat was far away and no one could see that I had finished, so I took my light stick and waved it into the air to show them that I was done, and on the French coast. *Bienvenue en France! Thank you, Lord, for bringing me safely across.*

The zodiac with the deckhand and cameraman took at least 5 minutes of rowing to catch up with me while I waited shivering on the beach. I thought to myself, *Not much use having a cameraman to capture a potential world record when the boat captain doesn't make sure his spotlight is working.* I wanted to swim back to the boat, but they insisted I take the slow-rowing zodiac back.

After climbing onto the boat everyone was fairly subdued until Diddo figured out that I had just become the fastest man to ever cross the Channel, setting a new men's world record of 8 hours and 12 minutes. This seemed to buoy everyone's spirits, and Coach Silvia was pretty emotional and got all choked up as he told me, "What a great swim, Paul." Having him with me was such a treasure.

Over the last six years there was no other person who had educated me more about marathon swimming, proper swim technique, and cold-water acclimatization than Coach Silvia. So much of my success to this point was directly due to his great coaching and I was so proud to have him with me for this record.

Once everyone knew that I was happy with the day the somber mood on the boat lifted and everyone relaxed. The emotion of an 8-hour-plus swim is very exhausting and they were all tired, too. Mike then started telling me that it was all my fault that I didn't break the record because I messed around in the first two hours, I ate too slowly, and other negative comments that infuriated most people on the boat. Very strange and uncalled for in the moment. For me, I just felt sorry for Mike feeling he needed to be defensive about not fulfilling his commitments regarding the zodiac engine and spotlight. I was just enjoying the knowledge of how fast I had swum and that no other marathon swimmer in the world could have won the day. There were many people who contributed to the success of today and I was very blessed to have their support.

Unlike most of Captain Mike's other escorts across the Channel, I had a lot of speed and experience, with 35 races of similar distance and many excellent boat captains along the way, and I knew the difference between a great escort captain and a distracted one. We also didn't make a point with him about how his lack of commitment to safety, putting me in a very precarious position by having me swim alone in the dark, or if we had needed the zodiac for a rescue. No spotlight, no working safety craft, no chart of my course—all unkept promises.

When we arrived back at the hotel I called my mom and dad; they were very happy. I also spoke with KCBS in San Francisco and they put me on live radio at 5:30 p.m., when there would be a high listening audience. It was all very exciting and a great way to end a fantastic summer journey.

The next day I called my mom's cousin Jackie Andrew in Kilmarnock, Scotland, as we had been writing letters to plan a visit after my Channel swim. We had never met or spoken on the phone before, and the call went something like this: "Hi, Uncle Jackie. This is Paul Asmuth from California."

"Aye, Paul, how 'bout that weather last night?"

This brought a great smile to my face as a big storm had come through all of Great Britain the night before, and he reminded me of mom's dad, Grandpa Andrew, who loved to talk about the weather.

No matter the records, swimming the English Channel was a wonderful experience. I was awarded a Rolex watch for the fastest time of the year. Sharing the experience with the Olympic Club and the South End Rowing Club, as well as my family and friends, when I returned home was a real-life highlight. Ernst & Whinney did a nice feature article in their international firm magazine, and now the cocktail conversations could keep flowing when I was asked, "Have you ever swum the English Channel?"

"Yes, as a matter of fact, I have."

Philip Rush broke the double crossing record that summer, on September 9, in an amazing 17 hours, 56 minutes.

My mom's parents emigrated from Scotland to Chicago in 1920, and the English Channel was always a very prominent body of water for them, especially for Grandpa, who crossed to fight in World War I. Mom let me know how proud they would have been, and I really felt that sense of pride when meeting Grandpa's brother, Great-Uncle Jimmie Andrew,

Uncle Jackie, and other relatives in Kilmarnock later that week. Thanks for watching out for me, Grandpa. What a blessing it was to have beautiful conditions and guardian angels watching over me.

Shakespeare Beach, Dover, Great Britain, proudly wearing Olympic Club sweatshirt
Photo courtesy of Diddo Clark

THE DOUBLE CROSSING
1985 AND 1989

In 1985, there were six tough and seasoned marathon swimmers who came to Roberval to try the first double-crossing race of Lac St. Jean, a distance of 64 kilometers (40 miles). The race would start at 10 p.m., proceed 17 miles across the frigid lake waters on a cool Quebec summer night, continue 3 miles up the even colder Peribonka River, and then turn around and swim back across the lake. This challenge presented the toughest conditions most of us had ever faced. None of us knew exactly how long it would take or who would be able to finish this beast of a swim. Only one of us had ever done the double crossing and that was Christine Cossette. The previous summer she became the first person ever to accomplish this amazing feat.

The excitement in 1955 must have been so similar to Christine's inaugural achievement. In the premier Lac St. Jean crossing event, Jacques Amyot, from Quebec City, was the only one out of seven starters to accomplish swimming across the lake in 11 hours and 32 minutes, a heroic exploit that most thought was completely impossible. When he was asked after the swim if he ever thought about quitting and getting into the boat, Amyot replied, "Well, I couldn't get into the boat that accompanied me because there was no room!"

Christine was a local marathon swimmer from Chicoutimi who

attempted the first ever double crossing of the lake. The local people were so excited about this new challenge that they followed her progress throughout the night and next day on live TV and radio broadcast. Over 10,000 adoring and screaming fans and hundreds of boats tooting their horns came to watch her finish in 18 hours and 27 minutes. An amazing exploit of athleticism and endurance that most thought was impossible. It was an incredible scene to witness and a fitting tribute to her accomplishment. The entire region of Lac St. Jean was abuzz with her triumph.

As I watched the year before this, the tremendous outpouring of love and support for their local hero, I dreaded what may come next for this race and the other eighteen marathon swimmers who were watching with me Christine's triumph. We were all going to be starting the 32-kilometer crossing the next morning and our feats would now be compared against this young provincial star who had just swum 64 kilometers. I shuddered to think that the race organizers would expect all future crossings to be 64 kilometers. However, the organizers were so wrapped up in the excitement of a swimmer being able to swim 40 miles and the unbridled enthusiasm this created, that changing to this new, incredible distance is exactly what they did.

Having a near-death experience in these water four years earlier gave me a lot of apprehension for this new competition distance. To date, my longest marathon swim had been almost 10 hours in Atlantic City, which was in very rough conditions and water temperatures varying between 65 and 80 degrees. But I knew the water temperatures in this lake would be in the low 60s and even colder in the Peribonka River when we had to swim upriver against the current to the halfway point, and that we would most likely be swimming 17, 18, or more hours. Daunting to even consider.

In addition, I had expressed my disappointment to the media about reducing the competitive field from the traditional 20 to 30 swimmers each year to six athletes. There were already too few marathon swims that paid good prize money to the athletes, and removing many swimmers from the most prestigious annual swim was a big deal. In the end I decided to compete. It was hard for me to pass up the possibility of winning the $20,000 first-place money.

My preparation for this summer's marathon swims went really well and I was swimming the fastest pool training times of my life. At twenty-eight-years old this was very promising for the races ahead and my first English Channel attempt in August. As a member of San Francisco's South End Rowing Club, I had done a lot of cold-water training in the bay's Aquatic Park cove and felt very well prepared for the distance and frigid waters.

The two weekends before the double crossing, I had competed in the 23-mile Atlantic City Around the Island Swim and *La Traversee du Lac Memphremagog*, a 42-kilometer (26 miles) race in southern Quebec, crossing the lake from Newport, Vermont, to Magog, Quebec. These races had left me a bit weary and with a sore left shoulder, but I was now accustomed to this pain as a marathon swimming "veteran," having competed in over 30 marathon swims in the prior five years. The 64-kilometer double crossing was an extreme challenge for me, and yet I also knew that I was much more prepared from cold-water training and racing experience than ever before.

Of all of the places that I had raced over these six seasons, Lac St. Jean continued to be my biggest nemesis due to the cold-water conditions. I had won the race twice, finished second another year, and not finished at all for two years. The only other competition that I had not finished was in Paspebiac, in my first year of racing, and then another year when no one finished due to extremely rough ocean conditions. Lac St. Jean continued to be my biggest adversary.

My brother John was with me again to help coach and guide me in the swim. He was a very calming influence and didn't get flustered during prerace preparations, at least he never showed his nervousness. Having been with me in this lake when I lost consciousness due to hypothermia, I'm sure this was on his mind a bit, too, as we began our preparations. We prayed again for safety and guidance in what was going to be a very long night and day.

The six swimmers and coaches gathered in a small room near the start dock to begin race preparations by applying lanolin to our skin on areas where we might chafe. We were then all called out into the night where thousands were waiting for us to start. As each of us were called there was a lot of cheering. I was so nervous when they announced my name, "Paul Asmuth, *des -Estas-Unis* (the United States)." I just wanted the swim to start so that I could calm down.

We jumped into the cold water and it felt so strange to be swimming in the dark. The lake water was already the color of black tea and now there was no light in the sky, either. I could see so little, nothing but black below and above me, the dimly lit spectators surrounding the dock all cheering for us, and the outlines of the escort, safety, and official boats. Each swimmer would have their guide boat and a safety craft throughout the swim.

As the starter counted down and shot the gun "*bang*," we started with a great splashing of arms and legs and swam out into the blackness of Lac St. Jean. Boat horns honked and people cheered as we left the safety of the harbor. Less than 5 minutes later, we were in the dead of night on the lake and I could see nothing except a small night light on my brother and the running lights of the guide boat and safety boat escorting me. Gone were the warm voices lifted into the night, wishing us on our way with "*Bonne chance*" (Good luck) and tooting boat horns, whose boat passengers remained in the safety of the harbor for a night of revelry.

I was alone, but not lonely. Another time to just be with my soul. A feeling now familiar to me after so many years of racing. The darkness quiets my spirit even more. Occasionally the search light from the safety boat or a bright flash light would hit my eyes and I would become temporarily "blinded," as my pupils were so dilated from the lack of light. What a bizarre experience to be swimming at night, very surreal.

The lake, as usual, was choppy and the going tough. Water conditions were predictably cold and I was swimming comfortably near the lead. Some swimmers had started a very fast pace, which I knew was not wise with 39 miles to finish—a long way to go.

Everything seemed to be going well for the first hour, and then my left shoulder began to hurt. This was a very bad sign with 37 miles to complete, but sometimes these pains work themselves out and don't become worse. John and our boat guide set an excellent course to keep me swimming straight, and the race organizers had placed big buoys with a blinking light every 1 kilometer across the lake to keep everyone on course. The Lac St. Jean race organizers have always done a great job of keeping the swimmers safe, and the guide buoys were a good idea.

While bothering me all week since the last race, I thought that perhaps my shoulder would loosen up after a couple of hours. But after two hours my left shoulder became very painful and now I was concerned about the other races and my first English Channel crossing attempt. Pushing myself too far could create an injury that would prevent me from racing the next weekend and missing the English Channel. With no improvement in my shoulder after 2½ hours, John and I talked and decided it was best for me to get out. I abandoned the swim after 2 hours and 45 minutes, knowing that I would not have been able to finish this time.

The next day I watched three of the six swimmers finish, with Claudio Plit from Argentina winning in 18 hours and 14 minutes. I watched him and the other swimmers suffer the last several hours from a boat, and knew that I would not have completed this double crossing. It was also a great accomplishment by Phillip Rush from New Zealand, coming in second only 5 minutes behind Claudio, and Monique Wildschut from the Netherlands, third in 19 hours and 5 minutes. Wow! Only three finishers; they were true gladiator heroes!

Seeing the condition of all their bodies after finishing also reinforced to me that I made the right decision. What I didn't expect was the backlash from the race organizers and the media, who vilified my efforts and made me feel very badly. Since I had not supported the new distance and then abandoned the race after "only" 2 hours and 45 minutes (8 or 9 miles of swimming at night in a cold lake), the press and race directors didn't think I had tried hard enough and criticized me in the press as well as personally. I had a tough time reading and hearing their very hurtful statements.

While the emotional pain of rejection from the race organizers of Lac St. Jean was very stinging and stayed with me that summer, I swam well the next weekend, winning in Paspebiac. Then I traveled to England and completed two successful English Channel crossings, setting a new men's world record of eight hours and twelve minutes. These successes after my abandoned Lac St. Jean attempt would not have been possible had I tried to swim further that night.

Over the years of competing in Roberval, I became friends with Denis Lebel, one of the race organizers. He went on to become mayor of Roberval and later was elected into the House of Commons of Canada from 2007 to 2017, where he held many ministerial positions during his term. Denis was always a supporter of the swimmers and had watched the *Traversee* since he was a young boy growing up on the lake.

An avid sportsman, hockey player, and cyclist, his enthusiasm and care for the marathon swimmers was abundant. Denis always had a smile and hug for us as he enthusiastically told us about some new development or project that he was working on, like the 160-mile bike path that he helped to successfully complete. The bike route wraps completely around Lac St. Jean and is known as the "Blueberry Route." The Saguenay region blueberries, chocolate-covered blueberries, and blueberry pies are world famous and deliciously ripe in July, when we would be there swimming. Denis would regularly come by other race competitions in Quebec to say hello and check in on his swimming "family," even when most of us weren't invited to Roberval anymore.

In the next few years my friendship with Denis would prove to be one of the most important relationships of my marathon swimming career; he was someone I always looked forward to seeing each Quebec summer. The Lac St. Jean race organizers declined to invite me to the 64-kilometer race the next summer. I was very upset, knowing that I was more than capable of completing this race when injury-free. The same thing happened the following year, which was again very hurtful, as I continued to win many races and deserved to be in the field of competitors. At this point I stopped asking to come; another summer went by with no invitation. I had moved on to stay focused on the other racing opportunities. Claudio Plit continued to win three more 64-kilometer races over these years.

Each of the summers after withdrawing from the 64-kilometer race, I won races in Quebec and around the world and earned one more international marathon swimming world championship. With these activities my name continued to be in the headlines of the Quebec media. During my years of banishment from Lac St. Jean, I never knew if the race organizers cared whether or not I ever competed in Roberval again. I soon found out that there was one race organizer and close friend from Roberval who did want me to come back: Denis Lebel.

Denis called me in the fall of 1988 and asked if I would be open to swimming the 64-kilometer event again. He knew that I had proven myself over the years and was now an excellent cold-water swimmer. While still never swimming a distance this long, I had swum in about 50 marathon competitions and solo swims over the last nine years. There were few in the sport with my experience and success competing at this time. I was thrilled with the invitation and began my nine months of preparation. While my friendship with and love for Denis was deep, I felt no such thing for the other race organizers. Nothing fueled my competitive spirit more at this time in my life than retribution.

By now my brother John had become the head swim coach at Auburn University and no longer free to help me in the boat. I knew that to complete and possibly win the double crossing I would need someone with vast experience in my boat. I called the person I knew could help me the most: Gilles Potvin. During the 1970s, Gilles coached John Kinsella to six consecutive victories across Lac St. Jean. I was grateful and also missed that Kinsella, a 1968, 1,500-meter Olympic silver medalist and 1972 Olympic gold medalist, had retired from the sport the year before I started. He would have been a formidable challenger.

Kinsella, at 6 feet 4 inches, was a very big and gifted athlete, with a commanding presence wherever he went. John learned to speak French, and with the Lac St. Jean and many other Quebec marathon swimming wins, he was loved by Québécois throughout the province. He was simply known as "*Le Roi*" (the King). Gilles Potvin is also a tall and strong man, and the physical presence of the two of them together was an intimidating force in any open water race. I wanted the experience of Gilles and the confidence that he would bring to my team. I was very grateful when he agreed to help me.

Gilles and I spoke often in the months leading up to that summer, and I included him on how my training was progressing. I would turn thirty-two years old just two weeks after the 64-kilometer race, and training days of 15,000 to 20,000 meters were much tougher for my body to recover from than at twenty-two years of age. Yet I was committed and focused to achieve something that very few in the world could ever do, and this intensity drove my training.

I lived in Santa Rosa at this time and trained often in the Russian River. Swimming upriver against the current helped prepare me for what it would be like swimming about 2 hours against the current of the Peribonka River. The Russian River was not nearly as cold, but surrounded by majestic and huge coast redwood trees over 200 feet tall and centuries old; it was the perfect place to absorb God's majesty and get ready. There was also an ideal little lake within Annandale State Park called Lake Ilsanjo. The lake is named after the former owner's wife and himself, Ilsa and Joe Coney—"Ilsanjo." A heartfelt story.

Lake Ilsanjo is located at the top of the park and about 600 meters across. I would run or mountain bike up "cardiac hill" and enter the water at a small dam. This was an idyllic place for me to train in the spring, while other venues were too cold. With only a fisherman in sight every now and then, I usually had the lake to myself.

In early June I left my work as a CPA with Pisenti & Brinker LLP for the summer and went to Santa Barbara, California, to begin my more serious workout period with Larry Liebowitz and the Santa Barbara swim team. Larry had been an assistant coach in Mission Viejo, California, during most of my years of training with the Nadadores and Mark Schubert. He knew me well and what it would take for me to be in top physical condition. I couldn't have asked for a better place to begin my hard practices for the long grind of a marathon swimming summer, especially with the hardest test of my career looming. In addition to being a great coach,

Larry had become a good friend and encourager, just what I needed in entering my tenth season of open water racing. He also knew I was on the budget plan and made room for me to stay in his home. I will always be grateful for his coaching and kindness.

Before leaving for Quebec I knew that I would need a significant period of cold-water preparation and spent two weeks swimming in Castle Lake, located near Mount Shasta, CA. This glacial lake, formed over 10,000 years ago, is part of the Sacramento River headwaters and ideal for cold marathon-swim training at 5,400 feet of elevation, water in the low 60s, and stunningly clear. Lots to look at during 2 -hour workouts.

The University of California at Davis has a limnological research station on the lake. Limnology is the study of inland waters (I had to look this one up). The lake is 1 kilometer long with a beautiful, slate-colored granite headwall at the south end rising up over 500 feet above the lake; it was perfect for long and cold, training swims. When stopped at the lake's north end, you can see the incredibly majestic Mount Shasta rising 14,000 feet and still covered with deep snow in late June.

On many days I was joined by a swimming friend from Santa Rosa, Bill Dick, who was going to be making an English Channel attempt later that summer. Bill had asked me to coach him in his preparation efforts and crossing attempt, and I agreed. It was also nice to have someone training at the same time in this remote location. While concerned about Bill's ability to complete the Channel crossing at forty-two years old, he was extremely diligent in his training efforts and never backed away from the challenging workouts I "suggested" for him.

After training in Castle Lake, Gilles and I decided that it would be best for me to come to Quebec early in July to train in Lac St. Jean and the Peribonka River, for as much cold-water acclimation as possible—a very good idea. We were much more concerned about the cold water than being able to swim the distance.

I arrived in Roberval and spent the first days there with Denis Lebel and his wife Danielle Girard. They had a small backyard pool to relax around; this was hoping there would be "warm" summer days to enjoy.

Summers can be very short this far north. Denis and Danielle's son Mathieu was a young, enthusiastic athlete, and we enjoyed time together while I taught him to swim in the backyard pool. A good distraction from the intensity of what was to come.

Gilles found me a small studio apartment in Peribonka from Mr. Paul Arthur Goulet. The room was located on the second floor, across the street from where the 32-kilometer crossing used to start and now was the halfway point in the swim. Still hard for me to comprehend, touching in Peribonka and then swimming back to Roberval? *Was I really ready?* I felt I was close.

Each day I would train 2 hours in the morning and 2 hours in the afternoon in the cold river that was a consistent 60 degrees. On some days Gilles would join me with his boat and we would swim to the mouth of the river and back, which would take about 2 hours. When Gilles was not there I trained next to the shore to stay safely away from the few boats that zoomed through.

Only French is spoken in most of this region and especially in tiny Peribonka. I had not mastered much of the language other than making sure I knew enough of what to order from a restaurant menu. Training 80,000 to 100,000 meters a week in cold water demands a lot of calories to fuel the body.

With no one to speak with, no TV, computer, or cell phone I enjoyed the quiet and read a lot of James Michener books. Solitude was my friend, and each day I felt stronger and more comfortable in the cold, dark water.

Before sleeping I would spend time visualizing winning the race and feeling what it was going to be like when I finished and won. The cheering crowds, boat horns honking, and Denis Lebel hugs; I wanted to make him proud. My heart rate would increase and goose bumps would rise on my skin as I continued to visualize how success would sound, smell, feel, and look like—bringing as many senses as possible into the picture to train my mind as much as my body.

The week before the 64-kilometer race in Lac St. Jean, I had committed to race in the 42-kilometer *La Traversee du Lac Memphremagog*. This was not ideal preparation for the 40 miles I would swim the next week, but with many friends in Magog and having won the race six previous years, it was very important to the race committee, community, and me to participate. I didn't want to rest as much as I normally would before a marathon swimming race and considered the event as part of my training for the 64 kilometers coming up the next week. With little rest, I swam sluggishly and finished fourth. While disappointed with my place, I felt on track for the next week and began my taper for the double crossing.

Cold-water acclimatization takes time. The human body is amazing for what it can adjust to when given a long enough phase. Besides training in the frigid river and icy lakes for more than a month, I had not taken any warm showers—the tap water in Quebec was very cold. In years past I had taken ice baths to help acclimate, trying to stay in longer and longer; tough stuff and no fun.

When first starting my marathon swimming career I was a poor cold-water swimmer, and now I was one of the better competitors in frigid temperatures. The cold-water training commitment during my first 64-kilometer attempt and English Channel crossings in 1985 helped me to understand what was needed for my body to fully acclimate. Thereafter, I performed well in races where the water temperatures were in the low 60 degrees.

Training in cold water is not enjoyable, and when done swimming, instead of running for the warm shower or hot Jacuzzi, the best thing to do is either towel off or take an icy shower. Definitely not for the faint of heart. Having the goal of achieving something special drove me to make sure that I was ready.

Gilles and I found a good fluid replacement and energy drink that we used during training for two weeks. We both knew that trying something new for the first time in a race—whether goggles, suit, cap, drink, etc.—is never a good idea. With this in mind we made sure that the drinks we would use were easy on my stomach, and they all worked well during the two weeks of prerace training in Lac St. Jean. I had never felt so prepared.

The race would start on Saturday night at 10 p.m., and there was a physical required before the race, on Friday. These were very routine at the races and a doctor took our blood pressure and listened to our heart and lungs. An EKG had to be sent in advance; there were no issues with mine. Normally I sailed right through these exams. This time, however, my blood pressure was very high; something around 155/90, and the doctor was concerned. I assured him that this was not normal for me but he would not clear me to swim. Wow, this was concerning and potentially a big bummer after so much preparation.

There was much discussion with the race organizers and subsequent blood-pressure testing and I was given the okay to swim, on the condition I signed a release of liability for the race organization and directors. In other words, if I died during the race my estate couldn't sue them for negligence. Knowing my blood pressure was only high because of my nerves, I signed the release.

This year there were eight competitors in the event for the first time, instead of six; maybe to make room for me? Not sure. Claudio Plit, the winner of the prior four years of 64 kilometers, was the clear favorite, along with Phillip Rush who had been either second or third these same years. The other athletes were Mohamed El Messery and Nasser El Shazly from Egypt, Alejandro Larriera from Argentina, Monique Wildschut from the Netherlands, and Nathalie Patenaude from Canada.

The night of the race was cold and windy at the start. There were thousands waiting to see us start and it reminded me of the start four years ago. It was great having Gilles in the ready room as I was so nervous, much more than other races, and I missed the calmness of my brother. I could tell that Gilles was nervous, too, as he began to spread lanolin on my body. We had never been together during a race and it was the one thing we couldn't simulate in our preparation.

Praying before the race I asked God to continue to give me strength and courage, to guide me and keep me and the other swimmers safe. To finish this race I knew that I would need extra strength, grit, stamina, fortitude, and belief in myself like no other time in my career. There was a reason I was back in this competition, and believed that God had changed hearts to make it happen. Now I wanted to be sure and perform up to my finest capabilities.

For many years I stayed with the Morin family in Roberval along with James Kegley. We had remained friends and it has been very heartwarming to watch their young children grow into adults, marry, and have their own children. On this night the Morin family was there for me at the start, along with many other friends, and Denis; I really felt loved by the community. While the race organizers may not have had my best interest in mind during the years I was absent from this competition, I could feel that the citizens of Roberval had never given up on me and were really glad to have me back.

After we were announced we all jumped in the water under the dim lights illuminating the harbor and held on to the small starting rope. The water was frigid and the air colder as the flags of the competitors' countries danced and snapped making a sound like distant firecrackers. This strong northwest wind concerned me. We were going to be swimming directly into the waves; it was going to be a long night and I was glad to be well prepared.

The starter gave us the countdown and we all took off swimming as his pistol went off. With all of our faces looking down into the dark water under the black sky, we could see nothing but the small boats around us. It always amazed me how fast many swimmers wanted to go at the start of these races that were 20 miles and more long, especially tonight. As we quickly exited the calm sheltered waters of the harbor, the lake instantly let us know that she would be in charge tonight.

Gilles was fast to find me and maneuver our small guide boat close by so that I could watch him for encouragement and the straightest course. As I swam near the front of the pack, near Claudio and Philip, I watched Nasser make a strong move to take the lead. The nighttime lake scene was surreal as we climbed over and through 3- to 4-foot surf, wave after wave pushing against us, and strong northwest winds blowing water spray from our strokes into the night air, softly backlit by the boat lights. Nasser was pushing hard. I let him go and stayed calm, pacing at 80 strokes a minute.

Stick with the plan, we have a long way to go. I was not having to work hard at all to stay with the leaders and felt at peace after the frantic start.

With each stroke I could feel the strong, cold winds blowing the water off my arms, back, and legs. It was as if the wind and water were trying to suck the heat right out of my body. I told myself, *Maintain stroke rhythm, heart rate, and keep generating heat. Stroke, stroke, breathe, stroke, stroke, breathe... Think of no one else, focus on nothing but stroke rhythm and breath.*

Through muscular effort I had my own internal furnace to keep me warm, as long as I could keep my effort high enough. The night was going to be extremely cold and tough. *Who would see the sun rise in the morning?*

Gilles and I were working well together, following our plan of feeding every 20 minutes. Having Gilles in the boat gave me great confidence; I wasn't concerned about our course and focused solely on swimming. Breathing, stroking, moving through the waves, breathing, stroking, moving through the waves, and now the hours began to pass. One hour, two hours, three hours, four hours, five hours...through the coal-black night we pushed.

One good thing about swimming in the dark is that time seemed to pass more quickly, with most of my senses shut down. No feeling, hearing, tasting except every 20 minutes—little to see, and the boats were downwind of me so nothing to smell. With all my senses suspended, all that remains is my soul, just me against the lake now.

I kept swimming the same comfortable pace and gradually began to pull away from the other swimmers. Over the last nine years, and almost fifty swims, there had been only a few times when I had felt this smooth and comfortable, despite the bitter wind and rough waves pushing against me. What a difference from the pain of so many swims. Even though I know that we still had a very long way to go; the athletic movements of this moment felt very good. I'm at peace in the storm.

With the lake being so far north there are about 15 hours of daylight each day. Sunset isn't until around 8:30 p.m. and the sun rises at 5 a.m. In between sunset and sunrise there are only a few hours of real blackness. At about 3 a.m. the sky started showing beautiful orange colors, and I began to feel the water temperature dropping. We were approaching the mouth of the Peribonka River.

Swimming closer to the river I began to see the forest lining the lake-shore, and there was a mist hanging over the river, eerily lit with the first light of dawn. I also began to feel very nauseous. Getting sick during marathon swims is not unusual, especially in saltwater races. However, this was something different, and I began to violently vomit into the water. I stopped to let Gilles know what was going on, and to my surprise, I could feel the soft sandy bottom on my feet. What a blessing it was to be able to stabilize myself for a few minutes while I continued to lose everything that was in my stomach. Rules allow for feet to touch the bottom during a race but cannot be used to propel forward, and I made sure that I didn't move while continuing to be sick.

This was a huge setback and I knew that I would not be able to continue if I couldn't keep my energy drinks down. By this time I had built up a large lead of more than 10 minutes on the rest of the field and had time to relax and evaluate the situation. I had been using this drink for two weeks during training with no problem. Gilles checked on the concoction. One of the ingredients had a dairy component and he quickly determined that all our drinks had soured, curdled, and gone bad. The warm mixture was meant to be consumed immediately, not sit in a heated container for hours. Big setback and huge downer!

I was in trouble on two fronts: Would my nausea pass? Could Gilles cobble together enough other energy drinks for the remaining twelve hours of swimming? Gilles encouraged me to swim, so I started swimming the 3 miles upriver against the current. The river's water temperature dropped as expected, and in this moment I was so glad to have spent extended training time in this exact location.

The winds suddenly calmed as the sun began to rise over the Peribonka River. The water was smooth as glass and the sun's reflection off the water was blinding as I slowly made my way toward the halfway point. I could clearly see Gilles now for the first time in 7 hours and watched his warm, foggy breath in the chilly morning air of 48 degrees. It had been a cold night.

While things weren't going really great in the moment I knew that I would at least swim to the halfway point and then decide what we would do. With the sun up and sky clear, it lifted my spirits as I sang my favorite morning song, "Oh, Happy Day" by the Edwin Hawkins Singers, to myself. The lyrics encouraged me to watch for God's goodness, fight hard, and pray. And that was exactly what I did—stroke, stroke, breathe, stroke, stroke, breathe—and kept heading up the river.

I didn't know what to expect as we approached the turnaround point at the Peribonka Marina and was blown away by the crowds who had been up all night partying and waiting for their swimmers to come. It was very uplifting, and I instantly knew that despite how I was feeling, there was no way I was going to get out of the water in front of all of these people. *Time to keep fighting and praying, with every stroke.*

Gilles encouraged me and told me we were about 1 mile ahead of second place as we entered the river. Looking back, I could see the other swimmers and they were much closer than 1 mile. Thankfully, I also knew that this shorter distance occurred because as I was the first one to start swimming against the current, my speed was slowed first and they were all able to reduce the gap between us. The time to catch me would still be the same as they began to swim against the current, too. No matter, I could see many of the swimmers' boats in what to me was too close and especially while not feeling well.

In the Peribonka Marina there was a board to touch for the swimmers, marking the halfway point. As I touched the board in a 32-kilometer crossing time of around 9 hours, I was happy with the time in the rough and cold conditions, and knew that I had been swimming fast at my relaxed pace during the night. Quickly turning to go downriver, my speed felt good being pushed with the current, and I rapidly built a larger distance against the closest swimmers while they continued against the current, a most excellent feeling.

The euphoria of the Peribonka crowds, and reaching the halfway point, quickly wore off. Now I started focusing on the fact that after swimming 9 hours, I had another 21-mile marathon swimming race in front of me to complete. Unbelievable!

Through all of the years of racing, I always tried to remember that whatever I was feeling, so was everyone else. If I was cold, tired, and sore, so were they. I pressed on, focusing only on the next 20 minutes.

Gilles hastily cobbled together what he could to sustain me—hot chocolate (yum), chocolate PowerBar, half of his ham sandwich (at least it was calories), and whatever else he could scrounge up from boats passing by. Time and motion began to blur; my body was numb and aching from the cold and fatigue. The pain in my shoulders and lower back was beginning to be unbearable—and the music was gone. *If I am hurting this much, so is everyone else*, I reminded myself, and focused on the next feed from Gilles, which occurred every 15 minutes now. After so many hours of pushing myself, all of my body's stored energy was spent. I needed more and more calories from my drinks to keep going, taking one painful stroke after another. Stroke, stroke, breathe, stroke, stroke, breathe… There was nothing left to feel; numbed and shivering from the cold, pain throughout my body, hour after hour of staring into the coffee-colored water and side of the boat, my thoughts were quiet. I was deeply in touch with my soul now, only stroking, breathing, fighting, and praying. And believing!

After the many workout hours during the prior nine months, Peribonka training regime of visualizing winning at the finish and hearing the crowds roar, there was no way my mind was going to let anything happen to the physical me, other than finishing and winning. In a great deal of pain, trembling with fatigue and cold, and running close to empty, I simply trusted in God and my preparation to bring me home.

Soon many boats began to come around me and I knew that we were getting closer to the finish. This was by far the hardest and most painful marathon swim I had ever attempted, and the lake delivered her challenges, from the very beginning and throughout. Thankfully the wind on the return trip was much less than the howling winds of the night, but now the boat waves caused turbulence as well-wishers raced out from shore at 25 miles per hour to find me. Once they spotted our boat they slowed, and their large, fast-moving boat waves washed over me. *Stay focused—stroke, stroke, breathe, stroke, stroke, breathe... Almost there, almost home.*

As we approached the Roberval harbor where we had started almost 17 hours before, there was a sea of crafts so thick that I couldn't see anything but boats. As we entered the harbor there were more than 10,000 cheering fans and over a hundred vessels anchored within the harbor for a close view of the finish. What an unbelievable feeling of love and support. I was arriving on the hopes and prayers of a whole community.

Gilles only had one request when I asked for his help. He said I always swam the last few strokes to the finish line with John Kinsella; would I be okay with this? I assured him that I would, and now I looked up to see this big man who had endured sitting in a tiny boat with nowhere to move for 17 hours standing up in our boat in his Speedo, ready to dive in with me for the last few strokes to the finish pad.

Gilles Potvin at the finish of the double crossing; boats with fans in the background
Photo courtesy of *La Traversee Internationale du Lac St. Jean*

As I touched the finish pad the feeling of relief washed over me like never before and I was overcome with emotion. The volume of cheers from the crowd were stunning, and something I had never experienced through the soft lens of pure exhaustion. I had done something that many thought impossible.

With many happy tears and hugs with Gilles, I felt that the love of the people had brought me across the lake and their spirits were lifting me right out of the water. I was feeling nothing in my physical body now, only the emotion of love; this must be what heaven will feel like every day.

At the finish after swimming 64 kilometers (40 miles) in 17 hours, 6 minutes
Photo courtesy of *La Traversee Internationale du Lac St. Jean*

The rescue divers helped me out of the water, to more hugs and tears of many on the dock, including the man who had brought me back, Denis Lebel. I think he was as happy as I was. My shoulders hurt so much I needed help to lift the victory trophy; I didn't care.

I had finished in a new record time of 17 hours and 6 minutes. Amazing! Thank you, Jesus, for bringing me safely home.

Finishing second was Monique Wildschut (17 hours, 28 minutes), third was Mohamed El Messery (17 hours, 47 minutes), fourth was Claudio Plit (18 hours, 48 minutes), and fifth was Nathalie Patenaude (19 hours, 19 minutes). Three of the eight were unable to conquer the challenge today.

This was the last year of the 64-kilometer event, and today the race continues with the historical distance of 32 kilometers. Maybe the race organizers figured if Paul Asmuth could swim the double crossing, then it wasn't so special anymore. The other marathon swimmers and I were grateful that they came to this decision.

A Tough Summer
1990

"Or let us also boast in our sufferings, knowing that suffering produces endurance, and endurance produces character, and character produces hope, and hope does not disappoint us, because God's love has been poured into our hearts through the Holy Spirit that has been given to us"

ROMANS 5:3–5, NEW REVISED STANDARD VERSION.

Being able to swim marathon races after ten years in the sport, and to be able to continue to pursue my passions after so many years, was such a great blessing in my life, and also a nice surprise. Most swimmers my age had all stopped competing after the 1980 Olympic boycott, or the 1984 Los Angeles Olympic Games. Still swimming extremely well in my eleventh summer after college graduation was a wonderful gift that I didn't take for granted. My summer "job" wasn't a job at all for me; to put away my business suit and tie and don a swimsuit, cap, and goggles for races around the world, and see old friends and make new ones, was an annual highlight of life.

After receiving prize money in my first professional marathon swimming race in 1980, the rules of USA swimming and the United States Olympic Committee prohibited me from competing as an amateur athlete.

After the 1988 Olympics, this rule changed and there was no longer a distinction between amateurs and professionals in swimming and most other Olympic sports.

The 1991 FINA World Aquatics Championships were going to be held in Perth, Australia, and for the first time there was going to be an open water swimming event, a 25-kilometer race. I was excited to be able to try to represent USA Swimming again. Since 1980, I had represented the USA around the world but always as "Paul Asmuth," an individual and not part of an "official" USA team.

The professional marathon swimming races had been my focus for the past ten summers. This season all of my training was geared toward the 25-kilometer (15½ miles) United States Swimming Open Water National Championships and the Open Water World Championship Swimming Trials in Seal Beach, California, which was held on July 21, 1990. The top two men and women in the race would travel to Perth and compete against the best open water swimmers in the world, and I wanted to be one of them.

Most of the marathon swimming races that I had competed in over the last ten years were more than 20 miles, and as this swim was shorter, I was still confident in my abilities. Although at this point in my marathon swimming career and almost thirty-three years old, I was no longer considered a medal contender, and knew that I would need to train very well to reach my goal.

In the spring I was contacted by a young reporter I knew, Ken McAlpine, who had written a couple of feature stories about me for different publications. He had pitched my story of trying to make the world championship team to *Sports Illustrated* and was hired for the job. Ken and I spent a lot of time together talking over the next couple of months, and he was always a pleasure to visit with. It was exciting to think that my story could end up in *SI*.

To help prepare for the summer of racing, I traveled to the Olympic Training Center (OTC) in Colorado Springs, Colorado, and joined Coach Mark Schubert who was the head coach of the University of Texas at

Austin women's swimming team. Mark and I had known each other since 1976, when I first moved to California to train with the Mission Viejo Nadadores, and I looked forward to training with one of the world's best distance coaches again.

The OTC opened in 1979 and is a converted Air Force base. At this time the dorms were just like sleeping in barracks. Bunk beds, bathrooms down the hall, and definitely not luxury. Thankfully, the cafeteria meals were excellent and geared toward offering a lot of healthy foods to athletes who needed thousands of daily calories. The United States Olympic Committee picked Colorado Springs as an Olympic training venue partially due to the benefits of training at altitude. The training center is at an altitude of approximately 6,000 feet.

Altitude training primarily helps athletes who are competing in mid to longer distance events that are more aerobic versus anaerobic in nature. Anaerobic athletic events are short sprints or have immediate exertion, like weight lifting or throwing the shot put. These quick bursts of energy require more oxygen to the muscles than the amount of oxygen that is available within the body's cardiovascular system, creating oxygen deficiency.

Aerobic exercise requires energy over a sustained period of time and the body uses glycogen stored in the liver and muscles along with fats as fuel. Physical exertion over 3 to 4 minutes in time are aerobic activities that use the body's stored energy as well as cardiovascular circulation to transmit oxygen and other nutrients to allow the muscle fibers to keep firing. Oxygen is transmitted to the muscles via red blood cells. Because of the lower oxygen levels at high altitude, the human body acclimates over time and produces more red blood cells to accommodate for normal oxygen levels in our system. When an athlete returns to sea level for a competition, the increased number of red blood cells carry more oxygen during the event, which can increase performance. This is why Mark's team and many other Olympic-caliber athletes come to the OTC for training camps.

Until your body has time to acclimate, training at altitude is much harder than sea level, and the adjustment takes some time. Typically, training camps last two to three weeks for the athlete to receive the full physiological benefits of high-altitude training. I would be there for eighteen days of training, and the first week was really rough.

At this time, there was no pool at the OTC and we traveled by bus to either a nearby outdoor 50-meter pool or to the United States Air Force Academy (USAFA) just north of Colorado Springs. The USAFA is located on a beautiful campus of 18,500 acres on the east side of the Rocky Mountains. Training at 6,000 feet in Colorado Springs was hard enough, and at the USAFA we looked at a huge sign on the pool wall that we could read when turning our head to breathe: "The air is rare at 7,258 feet." Yes, it is. Training 1,200 feet higher than Colorado Springs was very challenging, and I "gasped" my way through the first week of workouts.

Our ten workouts a week were typically 7,000 to 9,000 meters, and we swam over 70,000 meters each week. Very tough training, and recovery at my age was not as quick as when I was twenty-three; I was sore, tired, and probably a little cranky, too. By the end of training camp I had dramatically improved my conditioning, and knew that I was getting close to being ready for the challenging marathon swimming season. I will always be grateful to Mark for allowing me to train with his team, and the Texas women swimmers, for making room for me in the pool lane and treating me like a teammate.

The day after arriving home I swam in a 2-mile open water race in Lake Berryessa, California. I will never forget the endurance and speed I had during the race from the benefits of altitude training, which made me feel like I couldn't swim fast enough to get out of breath. Almost like a flying fish skimming over the tops of the waves. Wow, I wished that I could feel this way all of the time.

Two weeks later I was in Italy for the 20-mile Capri to Naples marathon race. I knew that I would swim well. The prior year I contracted a stomach flu the night before the race, was sick throughout the swim, and finished a disappointing seventh place. Having won the race three previous times, I was very disappointed and anxious to get back to winning again, if possible.

The first few hours after the start went really well. I felt great swimming in the front, then in the second half of the race I ran out of energy and finished third, which was disheartening given the shape I was in from my training. I felt that I may not have rested enough, and could just have been a bit tired from intercontinental travel. With marathon swims being so long, being physically off just a little bit can add up to a lot of time over the day; 30 seconds slower per mile is a 10-minute loss over 20 miles. Time to go home for the final push before the world championship trials.

Back in California I really felt powerful during my Mission Viejo pool training, and Corona Del Mar ocean swims, and knew that I was ready for a good race. I met with a young man, assigned to me by the race organizers, who would guide me during the race from his kayak. We had never met before, but I was impressed with his local knowledge of the Seal Beach waters and his kayak experience. We practiced once together before the race and found a nice rhythm for our feeding schedule.

The race started out well and I was able to take the lead, along with Chad Hundeby, from Irvine, California, a Southern Methodist University NCAA All-American distance swimmer and renowned distance pool trainer who had won previous USA Swimming long distance national championships. I felt really good and we set a fairly fast pace. Water temperature was in the low 70s and sea conditions were typical, with some choppy waves; nothing unusual for me.

After about 2 hours of swimming I began to feel fatigued, similar to how I had felt in Italy, and couldn't hold the pace any longer. As I slowed over the next 3 hours, Chad pulled away from me, and then another swimmer, Jay Wilkerson from Florida State University, passed me. It was a very disappointing day, finishing third in 5 hours and 18 minutes. What a letdown, knowing that my preparations had gone so well, and not being able to understand why my body was not responding like other years. *Am I getting too old for this?* I thought.

After more than 50 marathon swims, I had never felt this way during competitions. There would be no trip to the world championships, and no *Sports Illustrated* article for me. I flew to Quebec City three days later for the 32-kilometer *La Traversee du Lac St. Jean* the next weekend. I was exhausted and now had no idea what to expect in the cold waters of Lac St. Jean.

When racing week to week in marathon swimming, there is very little to do between swims except recover from the previous race. Increasing training to a level that causes additional muscle fatigue, or slows recovery from the previous race, is a mistake. I knew to train very little and rest. Each day I swam for about 30 minutes in preparation for the race on Sunday.

Lac St. Jean is always one of the toughest marathon swimming races due to the distance, cold temperatures, and rough waters. The crossing had been changed from the prior year's 64-kilometer (40 miles) double lake crossing to an extended one-way crossing of 40 kilometers (25 miles). Historically the distance has been 32 kilometers (21 miles), with the exception of the double crossing years.

The entire race was a slog for me and I never felt good, like swimming through the mud. I felt very flat and tired, finishing in 10 hours and 1 minute, a distant fifth place—over 40 minutes behind the winner Diego Degano, a new and very talented young stud from Argentina. Finishing fifth was tough enough, but finishing behind athletes I normally beat was humbling and frustrating.

After returning home, my three-year-old daughter Kendall helped put life back into perspective with her hugs and kisses, and letting me know that "It's okay, Daddy, letting the other boys win sometimes is nice."

Knowing something wasn't quite right with my body, I decided to see the doctor for blood work, hoping to find answers for why I was feeling so fatigued, and swimming poorly for the last few weeks after great training the months before. I had the final race of the summer in Atlantic City, and after seeing my blood-work results, the doctor told me not to go. He said that I was recovering from a viral infection and needed rest. At least I now knew that my physical fatigue was not psychologically related, and helped to explain my poor performances.

There really wasn't anything for me to do but maintain my fitness level, and see if I began to feel any better before Atlantic City, only three weeks after Lac St. Jean. I dropped my training down to about 30,000 meters each week, with only two longer swims in Lake Ilsanjo, a week apart.

I decided to swim in the last race and see how it would go. After arriving in Atlantic City, I met with my coach, Carl Smallwood, who had been in my boat the previous four years, to say that it had been a tough summer. I shared with Carl that I was in great shape, but that there had been a setback, and that I was there to swim the best I could.

After arriving on Wednesday for the Sunday race I was still fatigued and needed rest. Each day I would swim with Carl at the Margate Beach for 15 to 30 minutes, enough to loosen up, and then rest all day on the couch, watching movies. Carl and his wife Gerri took great care of me during the week, making sure that I got as much rest as I could. Not having won the race in 1988 or 1989, there was little prerace pressure from the media and I could relax. No one expected I would do much after my summer's results so far. I wasn't sure, either.

Based on when high and low tides were going to be on race day, we knew that the currents going out at the race start, coming back into the back bay in Longport, and finishing the race were going to be very difficult for all of the swimmers and rowers. The conditions were shaping up to possibly be the toughest ever. Exactly what I didn't need this year.

Carl and I spent time scouting out the critical inlet locations in Atlantic City and Longport before the race so we would know exactly where I would swim in each location against the currents; this knowledge would be critical. Making a small mistake while swimming against water moving at 2 miles per hour or more in the opposite direction can quickly balloon into a problem that changes the outcome of a race. Not to mention push me into something that could hurt my body. Over the years, I had learned not to take chances when swimming against current.

The race was full of great swimmers, including the prior year's winner David Alleva (a University of Virginia NCAA All-American), Rob Schmidt (a University of California at Berkeley NCAA All-American and a relatively newcomer to the racing circuit), and Diego Degano from Argentina. All of them had won big-time races in the past and were about ten years younger than me. Rob spent the summer working for the Atlantic City Beach Patrol and had the most time to prepare for the battle in race-like conditions. James Kegley was also in the competiton; he had started racing the same year as me, a wily veteran, and always a threat.

On race morning, Carl's son, Carl Jr., a Margate Beach Patrol lifeguard, was helping to row the lifeguard dory today, along with Wayne Coleman, a Ventnor City lifeguard who went on to play in the NFL. These young bucks with chiseled and tanned muscles were experienced oarsmen, just what we would need today. Coach Carl, who was the captain of the Margate Beach Patrol, was also good on the oars. Today was going to be a grueling marathon row as well, and a great team in the boat can make a huge difference.

The World Championship Ocean Marathon Swim as the race was now known (I always liked the original "Around the Island Swim" name) started in the back bay at Harrah's Marina Hotel Casino, across from Historic Gardner's Basin, where the start was for many years. Today it was interesting for me. I was more nervous about not knowing how I was going to feel during the race, versus nervousness about the competition. Especially knowing that the currents were going to make for a very long and punishing day. I felt no pressure from the competitors or the media; no one expected me to challenge this new, young generation of athletes.

It was so interesting to compare the competitors at this year's start to those in my first race in Atlantic City a decade earlier. Today the athletes were strong, trim, and fast. Ten years ago there was a combination of body types; even Claudio Plit, who was three years older than me and still racing, had lost 20 pounds and dramatically improved his speed. This year, everyone had shaved down their body for maximum performance; in 1980, I was the only one. The athletes had rapidly evolved for the sport in a short span of time.

When the starter's pistol went off there were twenty-three primed competitors trying to swim around Absecon Island in 9 hours or more, and we all took off in a rush to get behind our lifeguard dories to draft. We all knew that the sooner we could get to our boats and start drafting, the faster we would go, and the straighter we would swim following our craft.

As we exited the marina and turned right toward the ocean, the currents were already pushing against us as we headed out to sea. The ocean water was cool, in the low 70s, and swells pitched the small boats and made staying behind them to draft much harder. I always love the scene of the tightly bunched boats, oars rhythmically moving, flags of each swimmer's country waving, and swimmers splashing water into the air as we headed out to sea. Never knowing when would be my last year racing, I took in the beauty of the moment and prayed. *Thank you, Lord, for giving me another season.* Certainly not what I had hoped for, but I was forever grateful to be able to embrace my passion for swimming.

Rob Schmidt took out the first part of the race very fast, and as we approached the open ocean the current was so strong we had to leave our boats and swim right next to the rock jetty. Waves pushed us into theboulders, and barnacles growing on the craggy rocks scratched and cut our skin. We were only 30 minutes into the race and already getting beat up by the sea; she would be cruel to us today.

Making slow headway as we worked our way against the current reminded me of the first race my mom came to see in 1982. She never liked the sport but wanted to show her support; she flew up from Florida to watch her first marathon swim. It was the beginning of my third season. To create a more dramatic start and finish, the race organizers decided that the race would start on the beach and the athletes would have to run and swim through the surf, swim around the island, navigate our way back through the breaking waves, and finish on the beach. What a disaster.

The currents punished us at the end of the race as we tried to make our way back out into the ocean; we were actually swimming in place at times. My mom had followed me all day, from the start, to the Longport Jetty, to each bridge we swam under, and now, after almost 9 hours, was on the rock jetty we had to get around to finish. Everyone was struggling and getting beat up against the rocks by the waves and current. As I breathed to the right I saw my mom standing on the jetty, cheering, "Go, Paul. Go, Paul." And I kept swimming. Then after many more minutes of effort I would look to the right and there was my mom, standing on the same rock, cheering; "Go,

Paul. Go, Paul." It was like a terrible déjà vu experience, only real. I wasn't moving. "Go, Paul. Go, Paul," she would cheer standing in place. How wonderful to have her support, and what a nightmare to be experiencing the torture of the moment. She had to be shocked and scared for me; I know I was. It was one of the hardest races I had ever completed, and my coach at that year's race, Sam Freas, had to help carry me out of the water.

Sam Freas: my coach, lifeguard, and inspiration at the finish of the brutal 1982 race
Photo credit: *The Press of Atlantic City and Gregg Kohl*

At the end of the Atlantic City rock jetty we all took a right turn and headed south toward Longport. There were now many casinos to look at along the Atlantic City Boardwalk, rising high and modern. Much had changed in this city, and it was very different than the old family-oriented boardwalk, or even from my first year here in 1980, when there were only three casinos. The large buildings seemed like forever to reach, and slow to pass, as we swam by at about three miles per hour.

Rob continued to push the pace and I let him go, wanting to conserve my energy and still not knowing how I was going to hold up later in the day. The Ventnor Pier is a little more than the halfway point of the 7-mile ocean leg of the swim, and Rob was 3 minutes ahead by this point. I was feeling pretty good and just kept relaxing into my stroke, focusing on the keel of the boat and drafting as efficiently as I could. A three-minute lead at this pace was more than 200 meters, and I knew that this was significant.

Carl was giving me updates on the dry erase board, and we were working well together again. Just after Ventnor, Carl informed me that we were slowly closing the gap on Schmidt—175 meters, then 150 meters. I kept my same pace, encouraged that the gap was shrinking. I also knew that distances can be deceiving when swimming in current. Rob may have been slowed by currents we had yet to encounter as we approached the Longport inlet, where the tide was already ebbing and the swiftly moving water was ripping out to sea.

Drafting behind lifeguard dory
Photo credit: *The Press of Atlantic City*

Maintaining my same pace, the gap continued to close, and now I was only 50 meters behind as we swam closer and closer to Longport. The Longport rock jetty was packed with fans waving American flags and cheering us on. As we approached the shore Rob's boat stayed a little farther away from the rocks than Carl and I had planned. Rounding the jetty, I was now only 10 meters back and gaining quickly as Rob's boat was farther out in stronger currents.

Just like we had envisioned and practiced, I turned in toward the inlet beach, swimming in water less than two feet deep. My hands were pulling through the sand as the waves were breaking around me. The water was too shallow for the boat. Carl and crew stayed out of the surf zone in deeper water, straining with all of their strength to move against the current. Schmidt's crew may have thought I was still with my boat, as they stayed out in the much stronger current, and by the time I turned into the back bay, I was now in the lead by 45 seconds.

Rounding the final rock jetty into the back bay, it felt like I was fighting against a water cannon (had someone left a fire hydrant open?). I knew that the time to swim faster was now, as Rob struggled with the same obstacle I had just come through and hopefully I could put some distance on him. With Carl banging the boat transom—*"bam, bam, bam, bam!"*—encouraging me to push the pace NOW, I concentrated on drafting and swimming as fast as I could. Stroke, stroke, breathe, stroke, stroke, breathe… Rob gathered himself after Longport and came charging after me, swimming very well.

I pushed the pace through the back bay communities of Longport, Margate, Ventnor, and Atlantic City, and my lead slowly grew. After swimming for almost 7 hours, my arms, legs, and back ached with pain, but I was happy to have my normal swimming energy back, unlike the prior three races (I guess being a couch potato for a week can be good sometimes). As we weaved our way through the small canal, I was encouraged to keep going by the thousands of fans on the jetties, bridges, and in backyards.

The back bay waters were warm and calm, and by focusing and pushing as hard as I could by the time we reached the Albany Avenue Bridge with about 6 miles to go, our lead over Schmidt had grown to 4 minutes. Under normal conditions we would swim this distance in about 2 hours, but today we knew the hardest part of the course was still before us. No lead was safe in these conditions.

By the time we reached the Absecon Boulevard Bridge, the tide had turned and was now flooding into the back bay with a new force. I hugged the grassy shoreline and swam in water as shallow as possible, with my hands raking through the mucky bottom. The heat from decomposing mud was radiating into the water and the sulphur smell of rotting grass filled my lungs. *Hard to get into the zone in this hot and smelly soup; not so nice around here.*

We pushed on. To try to stay out of the cruel currents, I swam alone next to the shore. The water is too shallow for the boat. Rob is still just behind us and mimicking our tactics.

In the middle of nowhere, along the grassy shore, miles from any homes, there suddenly stood two steadfast fans who were always in this same spot, year after year, and I quickly waved to thank them (no time to dillydally). They had a sign that they waved back and forth: "Go, Paul Asmuth." I will always remember and appreciate the long walk they took to cheer me on in this remote area, with horseflies buzzing everywhere. A very special sacrifice for me, and great encouragement.

Paul, Logan, and very special fans who stood at the same spot in each one of my Atlantic City races, their encouraging cheers and signs helped me more than they will ever know. Bless you!

As we approach Harrah's Resort, there are piers and docked boats that extend out into the water. I'm barely moving forward, and upon reaching the docks, I realize that the water is rushing so fast that I cannot make it through. I yell to Carl, "I can't swim against the current. I will have to pull myself around." Carl quickly gets permission from the race director, Jack Garrity, and I begin pulling myself around the first dock, hand over hand, from pier to pier.

Suddenly my lead over Rob is less than 2 minutes, as his boat is able to watch what I was doing and not waste time figuring out the solutions. There was a 60-foot-long catamaran along the outside dock and we decided I would need to swim underneath the boat by myself, between the two big hulls, which was frightening. I slowly inched my way forward underneath the large craft, fighting against the rushing water, with nothing to hold on to if needed.

Just before the Brigantine Boulevard Bridge, there was a final dock filled with boats that I needed to make my way around, and the only way I could move forward was hand over hand along the dock or boat transoms. Now I was scared. This was no longer just about swimming, this was surviving. One slip and I might be sucked under the dock or boat. Rob was only 50 meters back and way too close.

As I tried to swim around the final dock the water pushed me under and toward a piling. I braced myself against the slimy and barnacled post, and pushed off to try to move forward. Carl yelled, "Don't do that or you will be disqualified!"

I yelled back, "I either push off or drown!"

Carl replied, "Okay, I guess pushing off is the thing to do."

I kept going.

I used every ounce of energy that I had left, and was able to get free from the last dock and swim behind the boat again. We all strained against the torrent of water trying to push us backwards to get under the bridge, and swim the final 500 meters into the marina finish line. The current was relentless, and I continued to strain along with my rowing crew. Swimming in these conditions took us an hour to go only 1 mile.

I was bruised and beaten from the rocks and barnacles that had scraped me during the race.

Stroke by stroke and foot by foot, we slowly crawled our way away from the bridge and into the marina, finishing in 9 hours and 54 minutes. Happy tears of gratefulness filled my goggles as I reached up to shake Carl's hand, and thank Carl Jr. and Wayne for the amazing job that they did.

Coach Carl Smallwood and Paul after 9 hours and
54 minutes of marathon swim racing
Photo credit: *The Press of Atlantic City*

Other than swimming the 40 miles of Lac St. Jean, it was the hardest swim of my life and the slowest winning time since 1964, more than 2 hours slower than my first win in 1980. Rob finished 2 minutes later, Degano 22 minutes after him, and Kegley another 9 minutes back. The prior year's winner, David Alleeva, was fifth in 10 hours, 42 minutes.

The conditions were so tough this day that only six swimmers finished the race.

Carl, Carl Jr., and Wayne were as exhausted as I was, and we all knew that today was special. Very special for me after such a tough summer of swimming, and extraordinary for them to be part of an amazing marathon, in the water and boat. This was my eighth and final victory in Atlantic City. Maybe the challenging currents this year were fitting. The water rushing past can be so much like our lives. After eleven seasons in the sport, time was rushing by for me, just like the water.

Watching the video of the live television coverage later was fascinating for me. To see the challenges that we had endured, and the end result, made the journey of the summer even more of a blessing. The summer didn't go the way I had hoped, and yet God had brought me through the storms and blessed me with another season of competitions, travel, and friendships. I was a grateful young man.

THE FIFTIETH
ANNIVERSARY RACE
2004

*L*a Traversee Internationale du Lac St. Jean is the longest-running marathon swim in the world. It has been continuously held since 1955, and 2004 would be the fiftieth anniversary of the race. The organizing committee takes their responsibility of hosting the world's most important marathon swim very seriously. The safety standards established by this race have become international guidelines in open water swimming events. The event is the "Super Bowl" of marathon races.

To win a Lac St. Jean race even once is a very big deal to a marathon swimmer, as well as the thousands of local people who follow the annual results. Over the years, many marathon swimmers have avoided Lac St. Jean because of her cold, rough water and river currents. To finish any crossing of the lake is a victory to cherish forever.

In my marathon swimming career I had been blessed to compete in ten Lac St. Jean races, winning three times, including the 64-kilometer double crossing (so ten competitions and eleven crossings!), and not making it across the lake three times due to injury and hypothermia. My last Lac St. Jean race was in 1992, and I had not done any cold-water swims of this distance since that time, yet I wanted to participate in the important fiftieth anniversary event. It would be a milestone event for the organization, the Saguenay-Lac-Saint-Jean region, and marathon swimmers around the world, both young and old. *Could I do this, or was I crazy?*

To think about the training it would take to complete a 21-mile cold-water crossing at forty-seven years old was mind-boggling and intimidating. The desire and motivation would have to come from another source other than me. I dedicated my training and preparation to my wife Marilyn, daughter Kendall, and son Logan. There was no way that I would be successful without their support, especially Marilyn.

The summer before, I had raced in the Capri–Napoli marathon swim from the Isle of Capri to Naples, Italy, a distance of 20 miles. The Bay of Naples water is comfortably warm and usually not too rough for the race. The buoyancy of salt water is also easier on the body and felt like I had just lost 20 pounds. The 2003 Capri to Naples swim went well and I had finished in good shape. The cold, dark waters of Lac St. Jean are a completely different beast, and I knew this all too intimately, having survived after falling unconscious from hypothermia in 1981. After twelve years of no cold-water swimming, would I be able to train at the level needed for success? Would my body be able to handle 50,000 to 60,000 meters a week of training, as well as cold-water acclimatization? Not sure. After spending time talking with Marilyn, we decided to go for it. When making a big decision, if we have peace regarding the process, we move forward.

Having recently swum the Capri–Napoli marathon, my fitness level was already good and I was able to carry this fit condition into the fall and winter training period. In the spring I began increasing my yardage, training in a small lake located at the base of the 4,342-foot Mount Saint Helena, the highest peak in Napa County. Robert Louis Stevenson and Fanny Vandegrift Osbourne spent their honeymoon on the mountain in 1880, and Stevenson wrote about this in his book, *The Silverado Squatters*.

The location is stunningly beautiful. When I breathe during early morning workouts, the view is stands of green Douglas fir and madrone trees, surrounded by bushes of manzanita and toyon tumbling down the western slopes. The lake fills each winter from rain runoff and the water is pristine and clear. The early morning spring air is around 50 degrees and the calm, glassy water 65 degrees—perfect for training. The owners (my friends), Bruce and Margery Meyer and their daughter Marguerite, have set up a 600-meter triangular swim course.

Margery began swimming masters competitions with Marguerite and the San Francisco Olympic Club when she was sixty-four years old, and went on to establish forty-seven world records over the next twenty-two years. She was inducted into the International Swimming Hall of Fame in 2009. Talk about inspiring! Margery loved to tell the story of when she asked for guidance on acclimating for a cold-water, 2-mile open water swim. I told her to spend time in her lake and only take cold showers. She would then tell the story: "Whenever I take a cold shower, I think of Paul Asmuth." We miss her quiet strength, determination, and wonderful sense of humor. Marguerite is also an accomplished athlete and continues to swim in many masters competitions and triathlons for the San Francisco Olympic Club.

The lake is about a 40-minute drive north from home. While traveling at dawn through the picturesque vineyards of the Napa Valley to work out, I would sing along with my favorite Christian music artists and plan my training. What a joy to have such a peaceful place to train.

In June, the lake began to warm and I knew that a colder training venue would be needed for my cold-water acclimatization. Good friends Tom and Marge Callinan had a cabin in the Sierra Nevada Mountains, on Gold Lake. The lake is filled with snow runoff, making the water very frigid and clear, with thin mountain air at 6,400 feet of altitude. I wasn't necessarily looking for any benefits that may come from altitude training, but the lake was perfect for cold-water acclimatization and Lac St. Jean preparations.

As often as I could get away for long weekends, I would drive to Gold Lake late Thursday after work, and train Friday, Saturday, Sunday, and early Monday morning, returning to work by noon. The first training days were extremely hard due to the 62-degree water. At first I shivered for longer periods of time after getting out of the workouts than I swam. Building up to two-hour workouts would take some time. Training in cold water is no fun and I had some big concerns about completing an icy 21-mile swim in less than a month.

I started wearing a heart-rate monitor during training swims to understand the relationship between my speed and exertion levels. The device also recorded time as well as high, low, and average heart rates. I found it very helpful in my preparation. It didn't take long for my heart rate to go above 160 beats per minute (bpm) while training in the reduced oxygen of our altitude. For my long swims of more than an hour, I was getting comfortable sustaining a good pace while keeping my pulse between 150 and 160 beats per minute. Day by day I got stronger and was able to swim farther. My body was getting used to the long, cold, distances again.

I knew that my training would need to be over 50,000 meters (more than 30 miles) per week, including many long, cold swims, and this was not easy to do in my forty-seventh year. My training speeds were slower and physical recovery took much longer than at twenty-seven years old; this was for sure. But my goal of going back and completing the crossing was different this time; I wasn't training to win but to share the joy of the journey with those I loved. What better motivation?

One of the greatest marathon swimmers of all time is Stephan Lecat from France. In the 1990s, Stephan dominated many races like Lac St. Jean, Atlantic City, and *La Traversee Internationale du Lac Memphremagog*. We had become friends in 1998, after I swam in Magog and Atlantic City. After the 2003 Capri–Napoli marathon, Marilyn and I vacationed in Paris for a few days and were able to share a meal with Stephan, his wife, and young family. One big thing that had changed since I professionally competed was that everyone was now wearing full-body suits in both the pool and open water races. This was something I had yet to try. Stephan assured me that these suits increased speed dramatically. I needed to wear one the next time I swam, and he gave me one of his suits with which to experiment.

I was still somewhat a skeptic, and decided to test the suit during a lake training swim at the Meyers' ranch. Typically, swimming a good effort loop around the triangular course, my time would be around eight minutes and 30 seconds. The first time I wore the full-body suit, I could feel that the material kept me warmer, and the suit's compression slimmed my body and made me feel sleeker. *Maybe this is how dolphins feel.*

After loosening up with a few laps and getting used to the suit's feel, I timed a lap: 7 minutes, 20 seconds. Wow! The suit made me go over a minute faster over a short distance? I was immediately convinced on the benefits of the new technology and began to more fully understand how international marathon and pool swimming world records were falling so dramatically.

I had done all of the training that my body could take and now it was time to go to Roberval and see what we could do. Marilyn had been so patient, kind, and encouraging of me during the toughest training periods, as I would get a little grumpy or discouraged at times with the pain and fatigue from the daily grind it required to put in the yardage needed to prepare for Lac St. Jean. She always knew the right thing to say and boost my spirits. We were ready. I hoped.

Stephan Lecat set the marathon swimming standard for many years, winning races and setting records, including the Lac St. Jean record of an astounding time of 6 hours 22 minutes in 2000. Stephan and a young Bulgarian named Petar Stoychev squared off many times in Lac St. Jean with first- and second-place finishes. In 2001, Petar won his first Lac St. Jean *Traversee* and went on to win ten more times in Roberval before retiring from his amazing career.

During his racing years I would see Petar from time to time; he loved to tell me when he had most recently broken any records that I had set, either fastest times or number of wins. When we arrived in Lac St. Jean for the fiftieth anniversary, his first comment to me in his thick Eastern European accent was, "Hey, Paul. I broke your masters swimming world record in the 1,500 meters."

I replied, "Petar, I haven't swum a pool competition in over twenty years."

Without hesitation, Petar said, "Well then I broke the record of the man who broke your record."

Ha! What a hoot. I looked it up later and found out that he would have had to say, "I broke the record of the man who broke the record of the man who broke your record."

Being around the other athletes, coaches, and race organizers was exciting for our family. I had not been in Roberval for twelve years and it felt good to be back. The race organization had built a beautiful new lakeside headquarters overlooking the harbor. From the second-floor deck you could see the entire finish area and many miles across the lake. On clear days you can see the land eighteen miles away, and where the Peribonka River enters the lake. The waters were the same menacing brown color and cold. I was very happy that I had spent so much time in frigid Gold Lake preparing. Would it be enough?

The heartfelt greetings that Marilyn, Kendall, Logan, and I received on our arrival were truly wonderful. People were meeting Marilyn for the first time and so pleased to see Kendall (eighteen) and Logan (fourteen), since they were only six and two years old on their last visit. We could really feel the love of the community and race organization. It was also so wonderful to reconnect with long-time friends like Gilles Potvin, Dr. Johanne Phillippe, and Denis Lebel.

The week was very busy with many publicity events and prerace meetings to attend, along with training and resting. I also wanted to show Team Asmuth some of the area, and we went to the *Zoo Sauvage de St-Felicien* (the St. Felicien Zoo). The zoo focuses on Nordic animals (Marilyn is Norwegian, so this was sure to be a hit) and also features the nature park trails where the Quebec wildlife roam free over 74 acres, and visitors ride in protected cars to observe them in a natural-habitat setting—an awe inspiring place.

The weeklong festivities of the competitive events include many activities for families and youth, including swims of 500-meter, 1,000-meter, 5-kilometer, and 10-kilometer events before the big 32-kilometer crossing. There are also parades and annual dinner in the street. The whole town is there for the Supper in the Street feast, serving the traditional *tourtiere* (Quebec meat pie), and the famous blueberry pie. There are thousands who celebrate at the tables more than 1 kilometer long, and dance and party late into the night. An amazing community event where all of the swimmers are introduced, mingle with VIPs, and sign lots of autographs. A very special moment to come back for and share with Team Asmuth.

Roberval's annual Supper in the Street
Photo courtesy of Steeve Tremblay and
La Traversee Internationale du Lac St. Jean

The week passed quickly and suddenly it was the day before the race. All of the swimmers were bussed to a former convent near the small town of Dolbeau-Mistassini for the night. After dinner I shaved my body and tried to rest. Morning arrived early after a restless night of sleep. I was really nervous and not sure about how I would handle the cold conditions or the 21-mile distance. Marilyn went about preparing our warm drinks for the long day ahead.

The morning greeted us with classic Lac St. Jean weather: rainy, cold, and wind blowing pretty hard out of the northwest. If I listened quietly, I could almost hear the lake say, "Welcome back, Paul." We would be swimming from north to south, so winds from the east or south were the worst as these gusts pushed big waves into our faces and made for a very long, tough day of swimming. The northwest wind shouldn't be too bad for us.

I encouraged Marilyn not to worry if my feet and lips started turning blue. Blood moves to the core to help retain temperature; she had never seen me look this way and needed to be prepared.

Even in the morning drizzle the crowds waiting at the Roberval Marina to see and cheer the swimmers off were as big as I had remembered. Good to see that the all-night partying tradition was still being carried on by some of the fans. With the summers so short in this part of Quebec, the locals like to take full advantage of the warmish weather. Being a Floridian this was not what I considered warm summer weather, and was more like a Florida winter rain.

There were twenty-eight swimmers to challenge the lake this morning—nineteen men and nine women from ten countries. I was the only USA swimmer and that felt strange to me; America has such a successful tradition in marathon swimming and it was disappointing not to have any other compatriots contending with me. It was such an honor to be representing my country and competing with this group of veterans; we were all standing on the stories, traditions, and legends of those who had gone before us. What a place.

There were several other past champions who got back into shape to challenge the lake this day, including Claudio Plit from Argentina (three years my senior), Robert Lachance from Quebec, Alexandre Leduc from Canada, and Irene Van Der Laan from the Netherlands. We were called the "*Anciens*" (ancients)—ouch, reality hurts sometimes.

The international governing body of swimming, known as FINA, started organizing open water races in 1991 with the first open water event held at the World Aquatics Championships in Perth, Australia. Since that time, there have been many FINA World Open Water Swimming Championships and other FINA-sanctioned races organized around the world, especially in Europe. The World Aquatics Championships started back in 1991 and was embraced by the European nations. There are now many experienced open water swimmers from Germany, France, Italy, Spain, Great Britain, the Netherlands, Greece, Russia, Hungary, Australia, New Zealand, Argentina, Brazil, Bulgaria, Canada, and the Czech Republic. This group of seasoned experts are very savvy and serious competitors at distances of 5 kilometers, 10 kilometers, and 25 kilometers. The USA has very few organized open water competitions at a similar level, and remains behind the racing experience of the European nations.

As part of all open water races, the technique of drafting behind other swimmers was now an accepted part of the sport, and swimmers swim closely bunched together in large packs for much of the races. Drafting is an advantage to the swimmers who learn the skill well, and really helps the women when both sexes start together, as they often draft off the faster men for many hours and miles. I knew how to draft but this had not been as much a part of my marathon-racing experience in the past; only within the short 1- and 2-mile lake and ocean swims in California.

As each of our names were called we left the warmth of the ready room to go out into the cold drizzle and greet the crowds that continued to grow as the race start approached. So many familiar faces in the crowds of well-wishers, including Gilles from Magog, who hosted our family at the 1998 race there.

Just before going into the ready room, photographer and friend Steeve Tremblay, snapped a great picture of Team Asmuth, and then I had to go get prepped. Marilyn then gently applied the gooey lanolin around my neck and underarms to prevent chafing. Afterward, we found a little quiet spot and prayed together for our safety and protection. I was so grateful that Marilyn would be in the boat with me today. What could be better to experience with your best friend? Well, there are more fun things to think about, like a Hawaiian vacation, but nothing as memorable.

Team Asmuth: Kendall, Logan, Paul, and Marilyn
Photo courtesy of Steeve Tremblay and *La Traversee Internationale du Lac St. Jean*

To be at the start on time, Kendall and Logan had to get up at around 5 a.m., but there were no complaints, only hugs and kisses. Having their love and support through this process and in the moment lifted my spirits. We didn't have much time together, and I know they understood. I couldn't wait to see them at the finish. Hopefully, I would be swimming to the finish line and not arriving in a safety boat wrapped in a warm blanket.

We were all called out of the ready room for the race start. Before walking out Marilyn and I shared a quick kiss and an "I love you," and then she left to get in our boat. With our skin exposed to the icy rain, the swimmers quickly paraded down to the dock's end and jumped into the river.

As usual, the Peribonka River held up to her reputation with water around 62 degrees and she took my breath away when I jumped in. Swimming in the full-body suit was helpful against the cold and I could immediately feel the difference. I swam around a bit, waiting for the starter's pistol to go off and trying to warm up. There really isn't much loosening of the body that works in frigid water other than swimming fast enough to get your heart rate up and muscles generating heat. Since the suit covered my chest I decided to wear the heart-rate monitor that I had been using.

The start was the expected chaos, with the swimmers' guide boats jockeying for position, race official boats maneuvering to keep the pleasure boats away for safety, fans in personal craft tooting horns, the flags of each country mounted on the guide boats flapping in the rainy breeze, and the shoreline and docks packed with cheering fans. An unrepeatable fiftieth-anniversary experience, and right now I was glad that I made the effort to come back and participate.

Finally, the gun sounded and we all took off upriver against the current for the first 400 meters. It always surprised me how fast everyone wanted to start a 21-mile race. I let the young, fast swimmers take off and tucked in at the back of the pack to draft. From experience, swimming these first 400 meters against the current always seems to take forever as we grind against the current, then we turned the corner and started flying downriver at more than 4 miles per hour.

The pace seemed fast to me (what did I expect?), and while swimming at the back of the pack was allowing me to stay with the fastest swimmers, it was also more difficult to be beside my boat for feedings, direction, information, and words Marilyn was writing on our dry erase board. She would share short phrases of love and encouragement, letting me know how proud she was of me—stroke count, "Looking good," "Strong and amazing", "I love you", "Denis on boat next to you waving,"

"Kendall and Logan on boat to left." What could be better than having Marilyn's full attention, love, and encouragement all day?

The water temperature was bitter, but I was feeling comfortable and grateful for all of my cold-waterpreparation. After about an hour I glanced down at my heart-monitor watch and saw that my heart rate was at 155 beats per minute. I knew that this was too high and unsustainable for the eight hours that I might be swimming. Although I felt strong, I quickly made a decision to leave the pack, swim next to my boat, and slow down a bit to allow my heart rate to go below 150 beats per minute.

Marilyn and I made a good team with her giving me my stroke rates, race info, and feeding routine every 20 minutes. There were a lot of swimmers ahead of me and many behind me so I felt in good position. The most important goal today for me was to finish, not to race.

There is pain that is unique to certain activities and marathon swimming brings distinctive agony after so many hours. At around 3 hours I started to feel the pain in my shoulders and lower back and had to start pausing occasionally to bend over underwater and stretch for a little relief. While I was well prepared, the conditions of Lac St. Jean were pushing the limits of my body and I knew this.

The day was cloudy, windy, and not warming up. After 3 hours my body wasn't warming up. I was cold and aching and began to question whether I had another 5 hours in me. I needed to relax and stay focused. Stroke, stroke, breathe, stroke, stroke breathe… Just swim for another 20 minutes until the next feed, and then just another 20 minutes, and then another. That's all I needed to do, swim 20 minutes. *I can do that*, I told myself.

Time becomes a blur when your senses are shut down. I couldn't see anything but Marilyn's smile, her red bandana, and her yellow rain poncho in my boat next to me, while never taking her beautiful blue eyes off me. The water is so dark, I can see nothing beneath me, not even my hands. There is no sun in the grey, overcast sky. My ear plugs help keep the cold water out of my ears, but also limit any communication. I can't see the other swimmers' boats and the rain has made the dry erase board only useful as a rain shield for Marilyn. My spirits and confidence to finish are low. Stroke, stroke, breathe, stroke, stroke, breathe... *Just swim another twenty minutes. I can make it. Kendall, Logan, and Marilyn will all be there at the finish and we will all be together.*

Exhaustion starts to creep in and my pace is slowing, which is not good for hypothermia, my biggest concern. It is important to be able to maintain a good heart rate so that my muscles can generate enough heat. I know this but there isn't much that I can do now except try to swim another 20 minutes. I'm getting cold and my body begins to shiver as I enter the early stages of hypothermia. (I'm glad I mentioned my blue feet to Marilyn; I'm sure they are that color now.)

As we come closer to the harbor there are now more boats coming around us to encourage me. The faster swimmers have likely already finished and the boats are coming back out onto the lake to cheer the remaining swimmers home. Then I see Kendall and Logan on a boat, cheering, and this makes me feel really good. With many boats and fans now rooting me along my sinking spirits are immediately buoyed. Stroke, stroke, breathe... *Just another twenty minutes. I can make it.*

I am close enough to see the harbor entrance; there are hundreds of people on the rock jetty cheering and many boats inside waiting with thousands of people in the stands, crammed along the shoreline. Coming into the harbor long after the faster swimmers I expected that many people would have gone home, but here they were—thousands of cheering fans—and I began to cry. Marilyn started to cry, too.

I tried to wave thank you and swim at the same time as I slowly completed the last 1,000 meters inside the harbor. Wow, what a feeling to come back to. I was buoyed by so much history, memory, and love.

When I touched the finish pad the roar from the crowd took me by surprise, and I waved as best I could to thank them. All I could think about in the moment was to swim over to the boat and give Marilyn a big kiss. The crowds loved that!

Perfect way to end the day with a forever-memory kiss from Marilyn
Photo courtesy of Steeve Tremblay and *La Traversee Internationale du Lac St. Jean*

Being helped onto the podium, the race organizers had made sure that Kendall and Logan would be on the finish platform to greet me. There were hugs, tears, and big smiles. I sat down and was wrapped in warm blankets. Marilyn was able to join us in a few minutes and there we were all together on the finish podium, celebrating together, just like I had dreamed.

Kendall, Paul, and Logan after 7 hours, 41 minutes of swimming across Lac St. Jean
Photo courtesy of Steeve Tremblay and *La Traversee Internationale du Lac St. Jean*

The next person to come over and give me a hug and kiss was the person who over the years has meant the most to me in Roberval, Denis Lebel. His love, friendship, and support is one of the main reasons I even considered coming back to try something I wasn't sure that I could accomplish.

Warm greetings at the finish from Denis Lebel on my left and Roger Gervais on my right
Photo courtesy of Steeve Tremblay and *La Traversee Internationale du Lac St. Jean*

My time of 7 hours and 41 minutes, and fourteenth-place man really didn't matter. The most important part was our journey together, and was absolutely worth the work and rewards. Thank you, dear God, for such an amazing day and forever memories.

Enduring Friendships
2006–2012

"To give anything less than your best is to sacrifice the gift."

—Steve Prefontaine

In 2006, the governing body of international swimming, FINA (*Federation Internationale de Natation*) along with the International Olympic Committee, agreed to add the sport of open water swimming back into the Olympics. The last Olympic open water swimming race was in the 1900 Paris Olympics, in the Seine River. The new Olympic distance would be 10 kilometers (6.2 miles) and would be called a "swimming marathon."

Some marathon swimming purists scoffed at a 6.2-mile swimming race being called a marathon. All of the "true" marathon swimming races around the world were 20 miles or longer. The more practical marathon swimming community embraced the opportunity to have open water swimming back in the Olympics, including me.

After swimming in my last marathon race in 2004, I felt a calling to coach in some way. I still had so much passion for the sport and would, in church, look at the back of a big, tall, lean young man and think, *Now there is a swimmer's physique.* Over the next couple of years Marilyn and I talked often about these promptings and I prayed that God would open the doors to which I was being called. Maybe the local team or an assistant high school coach; I was hoping for something local that would fit within my work schedule and responsibilities. God's plans were so much bigger than my small ideas.

Mark Schubert, my former swim coach from the Mission Viejo Nadadores, had recently left USC as the head men's and women's swim coach to become the new USA Swimming national team director. I called Mark in the spring of 2006 to congratulate him on his new position. Later in the call, we briefly discussed the new Olympic open water swimming event and Mark asked me if I would help advise him on the open water national team.

Mark first asked if I would help out at the USA Swimming open water national championships in Fort Myers, Florida. Having grown up in Fort Myers I was thrilled to be able to go, help coach some great swimmers, and visit childhood friends.

Mark then invited me to come to the Pan Pacific Swimming Championships in Victoria, British Columbia, to act as an observer of the open water event and the USA team. The gold medal in the men's race was won by Charles "Chip" Peterson, the race favorite, who had won the 5-kilometer and 10-kilometer events at the 2005 World Open Water Swimming Championships in Montreal at sixteen years old. The silver medal was a surprise, and won by Fran Crippen, a pool distance swimmer from Conshohocken, Pennsylvania, who trained with the legendary Coach Richard Shoulberg at Germantown Academy.

The women's gold medal was won by young, fifteen-year-old Chloe Sutton, and Kalyn Keller, an NCAA champion from USC, won the silver medal just 4 seconds behind Chloe and was now hooked on the sport of open water swimming.

After the Pan Pacific Swimming Championships, Mark asked if I could attend the World Open Water Swimming Championships in Naples, Italy, the following month and be his "eyes and ears" as to how Team USA was doing. Italy? Naples? Sure. I had raced 7 times in the 20-mile Capri to Naples marathon, most recently in 2003. I knew these waters well and thought I could be helpful to Team USA.

As it turned out, the USA Swimming open water coaches for the last many years had a competition routine that they favored for the national team athletes. Despite my twenty-plus years in the sport, seven world championships, and sixty-plus marathon swims, I didn't fit well with their plans. I was happy to help in any way I could, even if it meant staying at the hotel with the athletes who weren't swimming that day, and bringing them over later to watch the competition. Being in Naples was great for me. I had friends there from the many years of competing in the Bay of Naples, and it was good to connect with them.

What I learned at this FINA Open Water Swimming World Championships was that Team USA wasn't very good on the international scene. We were not even close to the commitment brought to the sport by the Russians, Germans, and Italians, and the results they achieved from their dedication was evident. What was the most concerning to me was that our athletes were ill prepared to race in rough, open water sea conditions. Team USA had a long way to go to compete against the best in the world.

After returning home I asked Mark how USA Swimming determined success. I will never forget his answer: "Paul, success is only determined by medals." I got it—no medals, no success.

In 2007, the swimming world championships were held in Melbourne, Australia, and the open water races at St. Kilda Beach. The water was cold, rough, and full of two types of jellyfish. Training in these water conditions was exactly what the team needed to be ready to race against the world's best.

One of the many jellyfish at St. Kilda is the blue blubber, which grows as large as twelve to eighteen inches long, and the big ones weigh about 5 pounds. When you run into one you really know it, because not only does it sting you, but the weight feels like someone or something has just "pushed" you; pretty freaky when swimming in the ocean. Thankfully, the sting from these "big boys" isn't too intense. The other jelly in the bay is a menace called lion's mane, and these have a very serious sting that feels like an electrical shock running through your body, along with a nasty rash lasting for hours. Thankfully, there were far fewer lion's mane jellys in the water. Having all of these jellyfish was still a serious issue to a team of swimmers with very little open water swimming experience.

Our women had a hard time adjusting to swimming with all of the jellyfish, and balked at continuing the open water training. To "share" the experience, I volunteered to swim with them, and they seemed encouraged by this. After a few days, jellyfish stings were no longer a concern. It was also a very good teaching opportunity, to remind the athletes that everyone would be swimming in the same conditions and that it was only their attitude toward the discomfort that mattered. We discussed that the one thing they always get to choose during their race (and in life), is our attitude.

After finishing our ocean workout one morning, we had a good laugh watching a newly arrived team of swimmers run from the beach into the water with unbridled glee. After swimming for just a few seconds, and seeing and feeling the stings of jellyfish, there were screams. They all turned quickly around and came swimming and running out in unison onto the beach screeching. It was quite a scene.

At the end of the competition Team USA had one silver medal won by Kalyn Keller in the 25-kilometer event; this was not success. Progress, yes; success, no.

The 2008 FINA World Open Water Swimming Championships in Seville, Spain, yielded slightly better results for Team USA. Mark Warkentin won a silver medal in the 25-kilometer event and qualified for the Beijing Olympics in the 10-kilometer race. The women did not qualify anyone for the 10-kilometer race, but Chloe Sutton won a bronze medal in the five-kilometer event.

Improvement, but still way behind the commitment and experience of Russia, Italy, the Netherlands, and Germany.

In May, Chloe qualified in a special qualification for the 2008 Beijing Olympics at the Olympic open water venue.

At the Olympics, Mark finished eighth and Chloe twenty-second, out of twenty-five swimmers. Not encouraging results.

The next year at the 2009 FINA Swimming World Championships in Rome, the open water competitions were held at the beach in Ostia, near the Fiumicino airport. This was the first Open Water World Championship for everyone on the team, yet there was a new toughness emerging from Team USA. Emily "Bruno" Brunneman, an NCAA distance champion, would swim the 5-kilometer and 10-kilometer events; Emily Hanson, an NCAA All-American and Bruno's teammate from the University of Michigan, would swim the 5-kilometer and 25-kilometer events; and Eva Fabian, the toughest fifteen-year-old I had ever met, the 10-kilometer and 25-kilometer races.

In Ostia, we started a new saying for the open water team: "Fiercest in the water, friendliest on the beach." It was time to start teaching these young athletes that they could be the toughest competitors in the water, and still show sincere care on the beach. One of our team goals was getting the host country to cheer for Team USA as the favored nation, after their own country's swimmers. I wanted our team to feel the love and support of everyone around them—at the hotel, beach, with interpreters, bus drivers, security personnel, the media, and everywhere they went. We gave out many USA Swimming pins and lots of smiles. It was wonderful to watch their confidence grow with this new attitude during the competition.

Somewhere during the first days of being in Ostia, I lost my USA white baseball hat that was part of our team uniform. The only other "official" hat I could wear was a funky, bucket-style hat that you see elderly men wear while fishing. A pretty ugly situation. With the blazing Italian summer sun I had no other option and wore the bucket hat every day. Fran Crippen thought that this was hysterical and spared me no grace in his critiques of my attire. It was a good daily laugh for all us in a highly charged, competitive atmosphere.

Fran and Andrew Gemmell qualified for the team in the 5-kilometer and 10-kilometer events. Alex Meyer and Sean Ryan would swim the

25-kilometer race. In the 5-kilometer race, Andrew and Fran swam really well, finishing in fifth and seventh, respectively. A good start against the best in the world.

Fran raced very tough and was out swimming everyone, but unable to hold a straight line. He kept going off course and had to correct his direction too much, losing ground to competitors every time. Fran was leading or up with the leaders the entire race. When I told him afterward that he was swimming faster than everyone else, but needed to learn to swim straight, he said something like, "Gee, Paul, thanks for letting me know," and stormed off muttering a few other choice words in my direction. Fran was bitterly disappointed; he was an ultracompetitive warrior focused on winning. My lesson was learning better timing for critiquing the performance of a gladiator. Luckily this moment did not occur 2,000 years ago in the Roman Coliseum, located just a few miles away.

The next day, Fran possibly used his anger in the 10-kilometer event and swam fantastically, along with Andrew, and was leading the race entering the final 50 meters, but went slightly left off course and struck the yellow buoy marking the entry to the finish chute, abruptly stopping him in the water. He quickly gathered himself, swam under the lane line marking the area, accelerated up to max speed to pass the other swimmers, and still managed to win the bronze medal, with Andrew taking the silver medal. Wow! Team USA was ecstatic! For the first time since Chip had won at the 2005 World Championships, the USA open water team was making some real progress.

The following day, Alex Meyer and Sean Ryan swam the 25-kilometer event. Alex was swimming in fourth position 500 meters from the finish, and was suddenly disqualified for accidently swimming over a female participant he was lapping and didn't see in his path. What a bummer for Alex, but he showed real potential for the sport and used this disappointment to fuel his passion for performing better in races over the next year.

While the women won no medals, they learned big lessons and showed a new toughness against the world's best, especially swimming in their first world championship competition.

To gain more racing experience, Alex, Fran, Bruno, and Hanson started competing in the FINA 10-kilometer World Cup open water race series around the world. This experience would prove to be both valuable and tragic.

In January 2010, the first race of this FINA circuit was in Santos, Brazil. When I arrived to help coach the USA athletes competing, Fran shared a book he had been reading, *Mindset: The New Psychology of Success*, by Carol S. Dweck, PhD. The book's pages were worn, with many highlighted and underlined sentences. He had spent a lot of time devouring the contents, learning how to train his mind for success, toughness, and a winning attitude. How great to see Fran's mature approach to success as he learned that mental training was perhaps even more important now than the physical preparation, especially in these elite athletic competitions. What an honor it was for me to be working with these young, determined swimmers.

In July 2010, the FINA Open Water World Championships were held in Roberval. Knowing the challenges of Lac St. Jean well, we arrived in Quebec City for an extended open water training camp and cold-water acclimatization. The goal was to get in a lot of open water training, acclimate the swimmers to some cold water, and then arrive in Roberval several days before the competition for even-colder water training. Quebec City is also a beautiful and historic place to visit and enjoy. The camp was a success for the athletes and coaches; what a blessing to experience the competitive life of this amazing team.

The previous summer in Ostia, Coach Jack Roach had taught the team that there are three main components to a successful team:

1. Time together
2. Common goals
3. Competition

We had all of these, and had definitely come together as a "team" over the last year. I would add that the fourth component is love. I watched how this group of athletes had truly grown to love, respect, and trust each other. Love can only come through trust, and it was such a joy to be around them and feel their connection. A real team and family.

When we arrived in Roberval our team trained in the lake every day, and sometimes twice a day for the 25-kilometer swimmers. It was interesting to watch the other countries primarily want to train in the pool, with the swimmers complaining the water was too cold, and the coaches being okay with this. It was the opposite of what was needed. Many of the world's best suffered with the cold in competition, and performed poorly.

Fran Crippen during the world championship training;
I'm wearing the ever fashionable bucket hat
Photo courtesy of Dr. Steve Hartsock

Team USA swam really well, winning three medals. Eva won the gold in the 5 kilometers, and Fran won the bronze. Alex won the gold in the 25 kilometers, and most everyone was in the top ten in their events. It was the best Team USA showing in a very long time. The final team standings for the Championship trophy: Italy, 116; USA, 111. Wow, only 5 points back. We had come a long way as a team.

Alex (left) getting a hug from Fran after winning the
25-kilometer World Championship gold medal
Photo courtesy of Dr. Steve Hartsock

Fran, Alex, Eva, Bruno, and Hanson swam in many races after Lac St. Jean, competing in Shantou and Hong Kong, China, Cancun, Mexico. And then in the last 10-kilometer race of 2010, Fran, Alex, Eva, and Christine Jennings competed in the extremely hot-water conditions of Fujairah, United Arab Emirates.

The San Francisco Giants and Philadelphia Phillies were in the baseball World Series together and Fran was a huge Phillies fan. He went to the game in Philadelphia and texted me to let me know he was there so I would know his team would be winning it all. I told him no way, and the banter continued. Fran left for the Fujairah race the next day.

On October 23, Bruno called our home in California at about 6 a.m., crying, and asking if I had heard about Fran. I said no. Sobbing, she let me know that Fran had died in the Fujairah race. I broke down crying at this unbelievable news. Marilyn and I tried to console each other as I experienced the biggest tragedy of my life. Our hearts ached as we thought about Pete and Pat Crippen, and their daughters Maddy, Claire, and

Teresa, as well as Coach Shoulberg, the German Town Academy family, the University of Virginia swimming community where Fran had been team captain, the Mission Viejo Nadadores, and the USA and international swimming body. All of our hearts were broken.

At the last minute, the race had been moved from Dubai to Fujairah by the race director and the FINA organization. Water in the new venue was too hot for competition, and reportedly was as warm as 90 degrees, with air temperatures in the high 90s or more. During the 10-kilometer race, Fran fell back from the leaders and told the coach on the feeding dock that he wasn't feeling well. Near the finish, Fran lost consciousness in the water, most likely from heat exhaustion, and drowned. There was inadequate safety and lifeguard personnel on the water and the surrounding course. No one witnessed his distress. When he failed to finish, everyone searched for Fran in a panic. His body was found 3 hours later, only 300 meters from the shore.

Almost all of the open water team, along with many from USA Swimming, the University of Virginia, and the German Town Academy gathered in Conshohocken one week later to support the Crippens and say good-bye to Fran. Everyone was in shock and deep grief. How to move on?

The open water team had some alone time together with a counselor as we tried to understand the tragedy. My faith in God is strong, and I had a lot of questions. I wasn't angry at God, just struggling to comprehend how this could have happened.

God, how does this fit into your plan? I trust you, Lord, but please help me to understand. Are you there, Lord? Can you hear me? Lord, I'm struggling and really need to feel your love right now. I will trust you, Lord, in the triumphs and the tragedies. Please quiet my soul.

Along with many others, I had never experienced such sadness and was besieged by my own grief, like the rest of the team. We were all aching in sorrow right now.

The 2012 Olympic qualification was going to be in Shanghai, China, in 2011, and we needed to move forward as a team, while still remembering the leadership that Fran had shown us over the last two years. He would want us to move on bravely. On the wall in Fran's room hung the quote from one of America's greatest distance runners, Steve Prefontaine: "To give anything less than your best is to sacrifice the gift."

I was most worried about Fran's best friend Alex, and grateful that he was so close with his Harvard University coach Tim Murphy and teammates. Fran and Alex had planned to go to the 2012 Olympics together; now Alex was carrying on Fran's dream for both of them, and his 2011 preparation showed what it is like when inspired to swim for someone other than yourself.

In an interview after Fran's death, Alex said this about their relationship:

"Fran was a fierce competitor, but he was also a compassionate teammate. On a couple occasions when I was struggling in a race, Fran would fall back behind the pack to check on me. Three days after I had swum the 25 km race at World Championships we were racing in a 10 km World Cup. Fran noticed I was swimming uncharacteristically and he stopped in the water and let me catch him. He asked if I was doing alright and he gave me one of his gel packs. A month later, I got very sick the day before the 10 km at the Pan Pacific Championships. This time I was even farther behind the pack, but he did the same thing. In fact he swam in the opposite direction on the course to check on me, and then he let me draft off him as he pulled me back to the pack. Most athletes would take advantage of a competitor being in distress; as much as I was a competitor, we were both USA, and he was a selfless teammate. These actions are very telling of the kind of person Fran was. He was one of my best friends, he took me under his wing, and he made me a better person."

There would be no denying Alex at the 2011 USA Swimming open water national championships in Fort Lauderdale, Florida, when he won the 10-kilometer event, qualifying for the Olympic qualifier in Shanghai. There was not a dry eye at the awards ceremony as Alex held on to a framed picture of Fran on the medals podium.

When Marilyn and I flew home the next day I wrote this prayer in my coaching journal:

> *"Thank you, Lord, for this beautiful woman sitting next to me. For her love of me, her laugh, and the light in her heart for you.*
>
> *Thank you for the opportunity to work with young athletes with big aspirations. Please direct my heart to teach them with your love and patience, and that I share your love with all.*
>
> *Thank you for bringing Fran and the Crippen family into my life. Open my heart to your will for making change and good out of Fran's life.*
>
> *Lord, I'm excited about the passions you have put in my heart; for Marilyn, Kendall, Logan, Meadowood, the Napa Valley Reserve, our home, family, coworkers, USA Swimming, friends new and old, and new ideas like Redwoods! Thank you for such a rich and blessed life!*
>
> *I surrender all and give all back to you!"*

At the world championships in Shanghai, Alex swam superbly and placed fourth, earning him his Olympic berth. The dream he and Fran shared was now his alone to complete.

Alex was fully devoted to his Olympic preparation and on track for a spectacular performance. In February, Alex called me from a Boston hospital, in tears. He had just had a bike accident on slick ice and fractured his collarbone. The injury would require surgery. What a heartbreaker.

After his surgery, Alex started training as soon as he could. Tim Murphy was brilliant in helping to devise exercises that Alex could do while out of the water for six weeks. When he could start swimming again, Alex was completely engaged to be competition-ready by the August Olympics, and he gradually gained strength.

On the Olympic race day, when Alex and I walked out to the water's edge, I told him to swim for love; that love is the strongest emotion and would sustain him better than anything. Alex swam a very good race that day, and finished in tenth place. The time out of the water had been too long for him to get back to the complete condition that he had been in the prior summer. While disappointed, I know that Alex felt he did all that he could have done to prepare, and so did all of the coaches, family, and friends around him. Fran was giving him his thumbs up from heaven.

Haley Anderson represented Team USA in the women's Olympic 10-kilometer race and swam magnificently, winning a silver medal. The team had come a long way during a difficult time.

The journey over the last two years had been a tough one for Alex, the Crippens, and the rest of the USA open water national team. There was a new USA Swimming national team director and my days with USA Swimming were over, as well. I was very grateful for all of the young athletes, coaches, and staff I had the opportunity to work with for the last six seasons.

Alex was young and had a lot more racing ahead of him. He was determined to improve at the 2016 Rio Olympics.

To honor Fran's life, the Crippens and other athletes close to the family started the Fran Crippen Elevation Foundation (FCEF), www.francrippen.org, a national nonprofit organization. "The FCEF acts as a central voice for safety in open water swimming, provides financial support through annual grants, and encourages the personal development of athletes through our humanitarian exchange program. Our branches work together to provide a full range of support to athletes who are committed to WORK THE DREAM."

Fran Crippen
Photo courtesy of TYR

ALEX'S MAGNUM OPUS
2016

As I watched Alex Meyer swim in the safety of the Roberval, Quebec harbor, I listened to the song "Beauty Will Rise" by Steven Curtis Chapman, a song and album written after the Chapman family had lost their daughter Maria to a tragic accident in 2006. The words about the joy that's coming in the morning and the beauty that will rise resonated with me today. I had listened to the healing lyrics of this album hundreds of time over the last six years, and I prayed that there would indeed be joy in the morning for Alex. This was going to be the final marathon swimming race of his career.

Alex, the Crippen family, teammates, coaches, and USA Swimming community had all lived through the tragedy of losing Fran Crippen in 2010. Now I watched Alex preparing to swim in the last major competition of his career, and the most challenging. Would this be a continued healing process for all of us?

The 32-kilometer (21 miles) *La Traversee Internationale du Lac St. Jean* is the most difficult marathon swimming race in the world. The race starts on the north side of the lake in the small village of Peribonka. The swimmers race the first 3 miles in the Peribonka River, whose waters are always in the low 60s, and then chart a course of eighteen miles across the lake. It was once ranked in the top five hardest endurance races in the world, along with the Tour de France and Hawaii's Ironman Triathlon. The cold water is one of the biggest reasons why completing the race is so difficult.

The race would be a transition for Alex, and for me, as we both continued to move through the grieving process for Fran six years later.

After the 2012 Olympics, Alex had continued to train for the 2016 games and committed himself to open water excellence. He medaled in many international competitions, including a silver medal in the 25-kilometer event at the Kazan, Russia, 2015 FINA world championships. To his great disappointment, he did not qualify for the 2016 Rio Olympics, and was now swimming in his last marathon swimming race.

Since 2010, Alex had traveled around the world competing, and always with him was a framed photo of Fran on the medal platform, holding his gold medal at the 2007 Pan American Games. Alex made sure to take a picture of himself and the photo together wherever he was. Fran and Alex continued to travel together, just like they dreamed. An amazing tribute to their friendship.

The morning of the swim dawned cold and cloudy with little wind on the river. Alex had trained very well in the months leading up to the swim and was diligent in his preparation. We were confident in his ability to swim 32 kilometers, as he had done 25-kilometer distances several times previously and was the fastest swimmer in the field. Alex wasn't too concerned about the cold river water, but silently I knew that this race would be the biggest physical and mental challenge of his life.

There were twenty-five swimmers in the ready room—sixteen men and nine women representing ten countries. There were many marathon swimming veterans in the race, like Angela Maurer from Germany and Damian Blome from Argentina, along with previous race winners Tomi Stefanovski from Macedonia and Xavier Desharnais from Canada. Alex would have to swim really well to win the race and bring his strongest determination and focus to conquer Lac St. Jean.

Alex was quiet, and confident, in the ready room. One of his best friends from Harvard, Jamie Mannion, was also there to help. Alex was a pro, and the routine of greasing with lanolin, and race introductions, very familiar to him. Denis Lebel was on the dock, wishing him well. We had spent a lot of time with Denis and his family during the prerace week, relaxing and training at his lakeside home. It was enjoyable for both Alex and me to be surrounded by supporting family, friends, and fans. Many of Alex's family had arrived along with his Harvard swimming buddies.

I left Alex to get in the boat, letting him know that he would be fine, and that I loved him. No hugs right now, I didn't want to get the sticky lanolin all over me. Once in the boat, Alex's mom Shawn handed me a bunch of American flags for a picture; all I wanted to do was get the race started. Taking a quiet moment before the race, I prayed for the safety of Alex, and the other swimmers, and my spirit was buoyed knowing that Marilyn was also praying at home.

The crowds were big, and loud, with television cameras, photographers, reporters, local celebrities, politicians, and fans everywhere. There were many Team Meyer supporters and American flags being waved. I knew that this support made Alex feel loved.

The swimmers came out on the dock and jumped into the icy 62.8-degree water. I knew that the lake may be as much as 5 degrees warmer than the river, and hoped we would find that "warm" water as soon as possible, because Alex was the least experienced in these frigid conditions, something with which I was deeply familiar.

The start went well for everyone as the swimmers navigated upriver for 400 meters against the current. Alex easily took the lead, and after about 10 minutes our boat was able to easily come alongside of him as they left the protected area and began swimming down the Peribonka River. We were with the current now and the water helped to swiftly push the athletes along.

At this point the pace was slow, and Alex was just relaxing in the lead. The slow speed allowed all of the swimmers to stay bunched closely together in one large pack. The escort boats were all jockeying for position next to their swimmer and there just wasn't enough room. Tempers were short as the small fiberglass boats kept bumping into each other like bumper cars at the fairgrounds.

Alex in the Peribonka River at the start of the race
Photo courtesy of Vicky Boutin

Alex asked me to take some pictures in the river while he was swimming, with Fran's picture in the frame. I did this early in the race while still in the river, to make sure to honor his request. Fran would always be with him and us.

We were clear on our feeding schedule of every 20 minutes and all seemed to be going well. I hung a thermometer in the water to monitor the temperature as the day went along. After about an hour Alex abruptly stopped, which caused all of the swimmers to deftly avoid him. As our boat stopped we were gently rammed by the surrounding guide boats.

"What's going on?" I asked Alex.

He said, "I'm okay, just need to stop and pee."

During marathon athletic events, athletes will often need to urinate. Colder water causes the breakdown of more stored body fats, which releases more water into the system, creating more urine than normal. This, along with the prerace hydration and slow pace, required an early need to urinate. Relaxing the bladder enough to eliminate while swimming is a challenging effort for many open water swimmers. When the body is cold and shivering this ordinary occurrence becomes a difficult experience for many.

Alex began swimming again and had fallen behind the pack by approximately 25 meters (about 75 feet). The pace continued to be slow and Alex quickly regained the lead. After an hour of racing, the water temperature was still a bone-chilling 63.2 degrees as we came to the mouth of the river and entered the lake.

Within every 30 minutes after Alex stopped the first time to eliminate, he had to stop again. Each time he fell back 25 meters and then moved up to the front of the pack fairly quickly. Two hours into the crossing the water temperature had only risen to 64.4 degrees; Alex was cold and beginning to shiver.

Around hour three, Alex stopped again and told me, "I'm just going to stay back here," meaning he was going to be swimming about 25 to 50 meters behind the leaders. At this point I could tell from Alex's skin color and body shivers that he was extremely cold. I was worried. He was without a doubt experiencing the first stages of hypothermia. Experience told me that the race pace was fairly slow, Alex's heart rate too low, and he was not generating enough body heat from physical exertion to stay warm. I knew if he stayed at the back of the pack, the next time he stopped he would be 75 or 100 meters from the leaders, and to lose contact with the leaders would be very bad psychologically and possibly the end of the swim for Alex.

I wrote on the dry erase board to Alex: "NO, we're going back up to the front of the pack" and "Pick up the pace," "Time to start swimming faster," knowing he had to start generating more body heat from muscle effort to avoid becoming more hypothermic. He was competition-ready and now was his time to get moving. The water was now at 65 degrees, the air no warmer, and still no sun. I turned away from Alex for a moment as I started to cry from deep concern and quickly texted Marilyn: *"Please pray. Alex is very cold."*

Skillfully swimming, Alex made his way back to the front of the pack and I told him to keep going at that pace. He began to move away from the other swimmers. An Italian swimmer, Edoardo Stochino, picked up his speed with Alex, and the two of them began to pull away from everyone else.

Alex was still very cold, but the extra effort and higher heart rate seemed to be helping him. I hoped that he would be able to keep this up for a while. Four hours into the race the water temperature finally jumped up to a "balmy" 68 degrees. *Thank you, Jesus!* I said to myself as the clouds cleared and I could feel the warmth of the sun on my face.

Alex and Edoardo had opened up a 400-meter lead on the rest of the field. Even though the water was warmer and the sun now shining, I knew that Alex was still cold, so I started writing him questions on the dry erase board to make sure he could easily understand me. A telling sign of entering deeper into hypothermia is confusion from a lack of mental cognition. Alex's showing a thumbs up or head nods helped calm my concerns regarding his hypothermia. A little while later, to check his perception and humor, instead of using "Stochino" when writing his competitor's position, I started substituting pasta names, i.e., "Fettuccini, Linguini, Spaghetti 100 meters back." It warmed my heart to see him smile a little. The water was 68 degrees and it was sunny; Alex was definitely feeling better.

Alex continued to swim strongly, and as we came within 1 hour of the finish, dozens of boats surrounded him and Edoardo, honking their horns and cheering them home. I would write notes on the board when someone he knew was nearby to encourage him. Stroke after painful stroke Alex kept up his pace until he pushed his lead over the Italian to 200 meters (more than 600 feet), and then I knew he would not catch us.

As we entered the shelter of the Roberval harbor, there were thousands of people cheering and boat horns honking for Alex. I couldn't help but cry tears of relief and elation, thanking God for his safe arrival, and for a moment, feeling the pure joy of Alex's victory and accomplishment. As he exited the water to the roar of the crowds, I loved watching him fall into the arms of the man who had brought me pure joy here, too, and now the same for Alex—Denis Lebel. Just like the song, beauty did indeed rise today, right out of the ashes.

Alex after winning the 32-kilometer crossing in 6 hours, 29 minutes, 59 seconds
Photo courtesy of Vicky Boutin

We will never fully recover from some of life's tragedies as we learn to live with our day-to-day "new normal." This is how it is for Alex, the Crippen family, and for all of us who love Fran. Taking ourselves beyond what we thought we were capable of, to "work the dream," as Fran loved to say, is our best way forward.

Looking at my favorite iTunes music list, the most listened-to song by far is "Long Way Home" by Steven Curtis Chapman. The lyrics talk about how, as we start out on our great adventure, we have no idea of how hard life can be, because along our journey the valleys are deeper and the mountains are steeper than we ever would have dreamed. How true.

What a blessing this life is, and all the unrepeatable experiences it contains. There are times when it truly does feel like a really long way home, and then other days, when we wish the water rushing past us would slow down because we don't want to miss a single moment. Life is like that. May God bless you on your journey, as we keep walking each other home.

Alex, Paul, and Ella relaxing in St. Helena with the framed picture of Fran Crippen

GOD'S GUIDING HAND
FOREVER

"And we know that in all things God works for the good of those who love him, who have been called according to his purpose."

ROMANS 8:28, NEW INTERNATIONAL VERSION

Looking back on life, it is easy to see how the decisions we made impacted our future. For me, the links between these choices have been Divine inspirations and appointments. Without my belief that God has a plan for my life, the odds of success seem very low.

How likely is it that all of these things would occur?

- An Olympic gold medal swimmer, Ginny Duenkel, came to our little Florida town to coach us when I was thirteen, inspired a new attitude in me, and required the team to learn one of the most important open water skills—bilateral breathing.
- The state record holder in my best event, Jeff Evans, joined our small club team at the same time as Ginny began coaching us; both pushed me to become a "committed" swimmer.
- Two years later, a new young coach, Gregg Troy, arrived and taught me the needed self-confidence and mental toughness I

was lacking, while making daily swim practice fun, which kept me loving the sport for many years.

- My Auburn University swim coach, Eddie Reese, encouraged me to take a year off after my freshman season to just train and physically mature, and opened the door for me to join the national champion Mission Viejo Nadadores in California.

- The Nadadores coach, Mark Schubert, made an exception (that he never did), and allowed me to train with his national team, even though I was the only one on the team who had never met the national championship qualifying times. He exposed me to powerful visualization techniques.

- Mark coached the world-record holder in my events, Brian Goodell. As we trained together, I gained confidence and learned that I could be as good as any other swimmer.

- Mission Viejo challenged me to swim over 100,000 meters (60 miles) a week, 5 hours a day, 6 days a week, for over 10 months, training my body and mind for what was to come only four years later.

- My Arizona State University swim coach, Ron Johnson, had coached the world-record holder in my event, the 1,500 meters. He taught me further visualization techniques and a true passion for swimming.

- While preparing for my first marathon swim, a coach from the University of Arkansas, Dr. Sam Freas, just happened to be in Mission Viejo for a swim meet and stopped me during practice to ask what I was doing. Sam then introduced me to Coach Charles Silvia. As it turned out, Coach Silvia was the foremost expert on stroke technique and marathon swimming, including coaching a world-record holder who crossed the English Channel.

- Sam Freas happened to be from the same area where my first marathon swim was to be held in Atlantic City. He knew how to row the lifeguard dory used in the race and agreed to be my coach.

- Coach Silvia knew exactly what was causing my shoulder pain and corrected my stroke technique, allowing me many more years of anatomically correct and pain-free swimming.

- The 1980 Olympic boycott pushed me to pursue other swimming opportunities before I started my first job after college graduation.

- In order to keep my swimming scholarship and continue training, I had to change my college major, from my passion of wildlife management to accounting for a career in the FBI. When becoming an FBI agent fell through, I ultimately received a job in public accounting (the last career I wanted in high school, ever!), which turned out to be one of the few professions that would allow my summers to be free for training, traveling, and racing for thirteen years after university graduation.

If I take out any one of these events or people in my life I may never have had the success in marathon swimming that I was blessed with, or maybe not competed in the sport at all. Coincidence? Luck? I don't believe so.

- Later in life my marathon swimming career and national and international relationships opened the door for me to offer experiences and coaching to the USA Swimming open water national team, and participate in the 2008 and 2012 Olympic Games and multiple world championships. What an honor to work with these talented and committed athletes and coaches. By chance? Probably not.

My wife Marilyn taught me a quote from Zig Ziglar years ago: "Success is when preparation meets opportunity." So true.

There are still some questions that will never be answered this side of heaven:

- In 1981, when I lost consciousness in Lac St. Jean after nine hours of swimming, why did God spare my life when many others have died in marathon swimming events?
- Were some of my achievements miracles or just Divine inspiration that I trusted and believed?
- Are miracles God's way of showing us that He is here with us?

Whatever the answers to these questions, and how the story of my life concludes, I know that I'm a blessed man, forever grateful for all who have loved me on this journey, even at times when it felt like "a long way home."

We all have things in our life we want to achieve or change, a story to tell, or something to do that may make a difference in someone else's life. What's keeping you from making that decision today? God loves you for even considering your options.

The poem "Footprints in the Sand" by Margaret Fishback Powers (http://www.footprints-inthe-sand.com/) brought me profound peace in my life in times of trouble. The poem talks about a man talking with God about his life while looking over footprints in the sand, and God telling him that they are the steps that represent his life. For most of the journey there are two sets of footprints, but the man is puzzled when he sees that during the lowest points of his life, there is only one set of footprints. He asks God, "Lord, when I needed you most, why was I all alone in my struggles?"

God replies, "You were never alone, my precious son. Those are the times when I carried you."

What I clearly know is that God loves us and has a plan for our lives.

After morning training in Lake Mission Viejo
Photo courtesy of *Swimming World* magazine

ACKNOWLEDGEMENTS

As with most young athletes, my first coaches were my mom and dad, helping to direct my swimming activities and develop my spiritual journey. Driving us to many 6 a.m. practices, weekend swim meets, and sitting in the Florida sun has surely earned them, and all swim parents, a special place in heaven. Both have been authors in their lives, which helped inspire me to share this book with you. Dad (Reverend Robert C. Asmuth) wrote about his chaplaincy with the Fort Myers Police Department in *Preacher with a Billy Club*. Mom (M. Violet Asmuth, PhD) wrote about her communication work in elder care facilities in *TLC: Talking, Listening, Compassion*, a training manual for health-care workers for the elderly.

The races and experiences that I chose to focus on in this book were the ones that were the most emotional and impactful for me over thirty-seven years. During my early career, it is important to acknowledge the support and contributions of Maura Campion; I will be forever grateful.

During my first thirteen years of serious and committed open water racing, I was blessed with much success. These achievements would never have been possible without the commitment, dedication, love, and friendships from coaches who taught me discipline, dedication, spiritual path, love for swimming, and then to be passionate about winning! My pool coaches, Wes Nott, Ginny Duenkel, Gregg Troy, Eddie Reese, Mark Schubert, Larry Liebowitz, Bud McAllister, Ron Johnson, John Meechum, and Duncan Scott, were the best any athlete could hope to have. There have been many more assistant coaches, trainers, and teachers who also made the journey successful, and you know who you are.

I'm also grateful for my teammates at the Fort Myers Swimming Association, Fort Myers High School, Auburn University, Mission Viejo Nadadores, Arizona State University, Santa Barbara Swim Club, and Bolles Sharks, who loved and encouraged me for three decades.

The San Francisco Olympic Club was a special place to train with teammates for over ten years, and the club was instrumental in supporting my open water racing and English Channel crossing. My good friend and teammate Don Hill told me that I was a "Clydesdale" in the water, and not to have aspirations to become a "thoroughbred" sprinter like him. Ha! I had no hope anyway.

The encouragement from my club-mates at the South End Rowing Club were highlights of long training days in San Francisco Bay's Aquatic Park while preparing for the English Channel. I especially loved my time with the late George Farnsworth. I could hear his booming voice from three blocks away as I walked near Ghirardelli Square. George loved to hear my marathon swimming stories; every time he retold a story about me, I got faster and better! We all need fans like him in our life.

The events wouldn't happen without great men and women race directors like Lello Barbuto, Denis Lebel, Eric Juneau, George Lussier, Arthur Lemarquand, Jean Dion, Serge Laurendeau, Yves Granmaison, Lynn Blouin, Martin Dussault, Bob Frolow, Jack Garrity, Dave McGillivray, Morty Berger, Roger Gervais, and so many more. They pour their hearts into making something special for their communities, swimmers, and fans.

Every race has an organizing committee to host the event. These are amazing volunteers who work endless hours to bring something special to their communities. There are so many to thank all over the world, and without them there would be no marathon swimming races.

At every location there were many media personnel who covered all the goings-on with genuine interest and hard work. I am especially grateful to Lello Barbuto, *Il Mattino*; Mike Shepherd, *The Press of Atlantic City*, Richard Chartier, *La Presse*, Rejan Tremblay, *Journal de Montreal*, *Journal de Quebec*, *Le Quotidien*, *La Tribune*, *Le Progres*, Moe Jacobs, the *Newport Daily News*, and Bertrand (Bert) Gosselin on Sherbrooke radio.

In almost every swim there was a boat alongside me, with an amazing person in it who was offering me encouragement, direction, and support; they are true heroes. They had to sit in small boats for endless hours in hot, cold, wet, and rough conditions and keep an upbeat attitude going all day, even when my demeanor might have soured. I am truly blessed to have had the greatest in my boat, including my wife Marilyn, my brother John, my sister Cindi, Sam Freas, Charles Silvia, Carl Smallwood, Gilles Potvin, Maura Campion, Kevin Campion, Brian Campion, Dr. Johanne Phillipe, Annick Lemarquand, Roberta Barbuto, Osama Momtaz, David and Susan Lang, Don Megerle, and Sylvain Hebert.

Boat captains kept me on course, protected me, read current charts, navigated in all types of weather, and had to listen to me harangue them all day long that they were too far away (back, forward, or too fast, slow, or didn't know where they were going). They were the best, especially Peppino Vuotto, Reg Brickell, Michael Oram, and Ron Kramer.

The men and women who competed with me over many years are the toughest group of athletes that I have ever known. I especially want to thank some of my many compatriots in the sport: James Kegley, Claudio Plit, Phillip Rush, Bill and Rob Schmidt, David Aleeva, Robert Lachance, Steve Munatones, Diego Degan, James Barry, Tom Wiley, Sid Cassidy, Corin Weinkofsky, Christine Cossette, Shelly Taylor, Monique Wildschut, Joke van Staveren, Irene van der Laan, and there are so many more amazing marathon swimmers over this time!

For the men and women who continued to push the sport of open water swimming forward over many decades—Dale Petranech, Sid Cassidy, Steve Munatones, Shelly Taylor, Lynn Blouin, Buck Dawson, Roger Parsons, Ray and Audrey Scott, Conrad Wennerberg, James Whelan, Major General Ahmed Zorkani, and countless other heroes of the sport

During these years I am very grateful to my colleagues and partners while working in public accounting at Kenneth Leventhal, Ernst & Whinney, and Pisenti & Brinker.

For my racing preparations in 2003, 2004, and while advising for the USA Swimming open water national and Olympic teams, Bill Harlan, the managing partner of The Napa Valley Reserve where I work, has been a huge supporter of my endeavors, and I am forever appreciative of his backing. The Swimming Hall of Fame reception honoring my induction for family and Napa Valley friends in 2010 from Bill and his wife Deborah at The Napa Valley Reserve, will always remain a special memory.

To the International Swimming Hall of Fame team of Brent Rutemiller, Bruce Wigo, Bob Duenkel, Meg Keller Marvin, and others; I thank them for their passion to recognize and preserve the global history of swimming, diving, and water polo.

During my years of working with USA Swimming, I am so thankful for the dedicated team that makes the travel, accommodations, logistics, and administration as seamless as possible for the athletes, coaches, and staff while we competed and traveled around the world. I will always appreciate the commitment by Candi MacConaugha, Deanna Paschal, Lindsay Mintenko, Bryce Elser, Michael Unger, Jack Roach, and Mark Schubert for the global experiences offered.

After my first thirteen years of professional marathon swimming races I was blessed to compete again in 1998, 2003, and 2004 with "Team Asmuth"—my wife Marilyn, daughter Kendall, and son Logan, who honored my swimming passions and desires to return to marathon swimming and share with them the sport I love so much. They supported my efforts and made it such a special gift of time together with them and friends around the world.

To the continued encouragement and support of the Elm Hill Books publishing team. I am grateful for their thoughtful and patient guidance of a first-time author.

Our friend, and accomplished author, Ken McAlpine read the original rough manuscript and offered his experienced insights, pushing me to go deeper and offer more of myself to you, the reader. His gentle and inspiring encouragement brought out more from each story and much more of me.

This book could be completely written just about the contributions and sacrifices of so many, and I am a grateful man for all of their support and sacrifices for my swimming, coaching, and faith voyage.

Through this journey I've learned that writing a book is a marathon, too—no sweating, but lots of tears.

Appendix

PAUL ASMUTH					
WORLD RECORD HISTORY					
EVENT	LOCATION	DATE	TIME	DISTANCE (miles)	
1 24-HOURS OF LA TUQUE (2-MAN RELAY)	LA TUQUE, QUEBEC	Jul-80	24 hours	69	(With James Kegley)
2 LA TRAVERSEE DU LAC MEMPHREMAGOG	MAGOG, QUEBEC	Aug-80	9h51m39s	26	
3 LES QUATORZE MILLES DE PASPEBIAC	PASPEBIAC, QUEBEC	Aug-81	5h35m	16	
4 LA TRAVERSEE DU LAC MEMPHREMAGOG	MAGOG, QUEBEC	Aug-81	8h48m22s	26	
5 CAPRI-NAPOLI	CAPRI, ITALY	Jul-82	6h35m	20	
6 LA TRAVERSEE DU LAC MEMPHREMAGOG	MAGOG, QUEBEC	Jul-83	8h34m17s	26	
7 SWIM AROUND MANHATTON ISLAND	NEW YORK, NEW YORK	Aug-83	6h49m	28*	
8 SWIMMING MARATHON OF LOS CABOS	CABO SAN LUCAS, MEXICO	Aug-84	8h12m	24	
9 LA TRAVERSEE DU LAC MEMPHREMAGOG	MAGOG, QUEBEC	Aug-85	8h29m31s	26	
10 ENGLAND - FRANCE, ENGLISH CHANNEL	DOVER, ENGLAND	Sep-85	8h12m	21*	(new Men's World Record)
11 NANTUCKET TO CAPE COD	NANTUCKET, MASSACHUSETS	Sep-86	12h1m	30*	(first & only crossing)
12 SWIMMING MARATHON OF CANCUN	CANCUN, MEXICO	Aug-87	8h41m	22	
13 LA TRAVERSEE DU LAC ST. JEAN	ROBERVAL, QEUBEC	Jul-89	17h6m	40	

*   Designates solo swim

PAUL ASMUTH
MARATHON SWIMMING RESULTS

EVENTS

WORLD PROFESSIONAL MARATHON SWIMMING CHAMPION (WC)		WC	WC	WC	WC	WC	WC			WC					
RACE LOCATION	DISTANCE (miles)	1980	1981	1982	1983	1984	1985	1986	1987	1988	1989	1990	1991	1992	TOTAL FIRST
ATLANTIC CITY, NEW JERSEY	23	1st	1st	1st	1st	1st	1st		1st	2nd	2nd	1st	4th	4th	8
LAC ST. JEAN, QUEBEC	21	1st	dnf	dnf	1st	2nd									2
LAC ST. JEAN, QUEBEC	40						dnf				1st				1
LAC ST. JEAN, QUEBEC	25											5th	6th	2nd	
LAC MEMPHREMAGOG, QUEBEC	26	1st	1st	1st	1st	3rd	1st	1st		3rd	4th		7th		6
PASPEBIAC, QUEBEC	16	dnf	1st	3rd	dnf	1st	1st	dnf		1st					4
LA TUQUE, QUEBEC (24 HR. RELAY)	69	1st													1
LA TUQUE, QUEBEC	15		1st												1
CAPRI - NAPOLI, ITALY	20								1st	1st	7th	3rd		10th	3
PORT SAID, EGYPT	21	1st		2nd											1
ALEXANDRIA, EGYPT	18	1st		2nd											1
ISMALIA, EGYPT	15			3rd											
NILE RIVER, EGYPT	18			2nd											
RAS-EL-BAR, EGYPT	20			2nd											
CABO SAN LUCAS, MEXICO	24					1st									1
CANCUN, MEXICO	24									1st					1
SEAL BEACH, CALIFORNIA	15											3rd			
MANHATTAN ISLAND, NEW YORK	28					1st									1

SUMMARY OF RESULTS

		1980	1981	1982	1983	1984	1985	1986	1987	1988	1989	1990	1991	1992	TOTAL
TOTAL FIRST PLACE		6	4	3	3	4	3	1	3	2	1	1			31
TOTAL SECOND PLACE				4		1				1	1		1		8
TOTAL THIRD PLACE				2		1				1		2	2		8
TOTAL OTHER		1	1	1	1		1	1			2	1	3		12
TOTALS		7	5	10	4	6	4	2	3	4	4	4	3	3	59

dnf - Did Not Finish

ABOUT THE AUTHOR

Paul Andrew Asmuth grew up in Fort Myers, Florida. He graduated from Fort Myers High School and then attended Auburn University for one year. He subsequently graduated from Arizona State University in 1980 with a bachelor of science degree in accounting. At Arizona State he was a three-time NCAA All-American swimmer and team cocaptain (1978–1980). After the 1980 Olympic boycott, he entered the sport of professional marathon swimming.

During the 1980s, Paul dominated professional marathon swimming races. He won seven World Professional Marathon Federation titles (1980–1985, 1988). During this time he competed in 59 races, winning 31 of them, including a record 8 times in the Atlantic City Around the Island Swim (23 miles); a record 6 times in *La Traversee du Lac Memphremagog* (26 miles), holding the record from 1980–1994; 4 times in *Les Quatorze Milles de Paspebiac* (16 miles), holding the record of 5 hours and 35 minutes; 3 times in the Capri to Naples marathon (20 miles) and held the record of 6 hours and 35 minutes from 1982–2012; and 3 times in *La Traversee du Lac St. Jean* (21 and 40 miles) and holds the 40-mile record of 17 hours and 6 minutes. In 1990, he was named the Athlete of the Decade by *The Press of Atlantic City*.

He also completed 3 English Channel crossings (21 miles), setting the men's world record of 8 hours and 12 minutes in 1985; became the first person to cross Nantucket Sound from Nantucket Island to Craigville

Beach, Cape Cod (24 miles) in 1986, 12 hours and 1 minute; and in 1983 was the first person to swim under 7 hours around Manhattan Island (28 miles), 6 hours and 49 minutes.

To bring the sport to life for his wife Marilyn, daughter Kendall, and son Logan, Paul competed again in races in *Lac Memphremagog* and in Atlantic City in 1998, Capri to Naples in 2003, and *Lac St. Jean* in 2004 (the fiftieth anniversary of the event).

Paul was inducted into the International Marathon Swimming Hall of Fame in 1982 and the International Swimming Hall of Fame in 2010.

Paul worked as a public accountant from 1980 to 1997, and was a California certified public accountant during this time. In 1993, he earned a master of science degree in taxation from Golden Gate University, San Francisco, California. Over his last ten years in the profession, he worked with Pisenti & Brinker LLP; he was a partner with the firm and in charge of the Napa, California, office.

From 2006 to 2012, he advised the USA Swimming open water national team and coached at the 2008 Beijing and 2012 London Olympics, six world championships, and multiple other events around the globe.

He is currently the general manager of The Napa Valley Reserve winery in St. Helena, California, where he has worked since July 2000, and also serves on the executive committee of Meadowood Napa Valley, an adjoining Relais & Chateaux, triple five-star Forbes resort.

Since early 2017, Paul has served on the vestry committee of Grace Episcopal Church where he worships. He also joined the board of directors of the Land Trust of Napa County during this year.

After seeing his first coast redwood tree in 1976, Paul developed a passion for these amazing and unique trees. He founded and manages a 475 coast redwood carbon-sequestration forest in St. Helena. This experimental planting is being irrigated with effluent from a nearby wastewater treatment plant.

He lives in St. Helena with his wife Marilyn. They met at Grace Episcopal Church and were married there in 1999.

9 781595 557742